Praise for *Leading Winni*

"*Leading Winning Teams* is an excellent guide and blueprint by a three-time MLB World Series coach for optimizing team dynamics and driving strategy and peak performance through development and enablement of good culture and leadership via principles of perseverance, positioning, and resiliency."

—**Mike Dempsey,**
NFL alumnus, Carolinas Chapter Board Member

"Just devoured *Leading Winning Teams* by Trent Clark. All I can say is one word: *revitalized.* I have been CEO of my company for 25 years and fired up to incorporate this life work from Trent's life. Just started playing on a men's baseball league two months ago at age 63 and going to give this book to all my teammates as a gift as soon as it's released!"

—**Mark Battiato,**
CEO, Growth Into Greatness Institute

"There are a lot of great recipes but most of them have the same core ingredients. Most chefs keep those ingredients secret. But Trent has done just the opposite with his book. Drawing from the experiences of many successful people in various walks of life including his own, Trent reveals those core ingredients that have contributed to the success of many folks. A must-read for anyone wanting to feast on the ingredients that have produced great recipes for success for many folks in various walks of life from business to sports."

—**Darrell T. Davies,**
professor of human anatomy and physiology, USTA and
ITA certified tennis official and referee for the USTA Boys 18s and
16s National Championships

"Exceptional insights on building winning teams! *Leading Winning Teams* is a guide that will resonate with leaders across industries. An inspiring read!"

—**Cary Chessick,**
founder of Restaurants.com, Rabine Technologies,
Rewards21, and Profitology; author of *Pitch Before Product*

"*Leading Winning Teams* is a game plan for ultimate success. Trent Clark leverages his experience at the highest level across sports and business to provide a roadmap for us to become leaders in whatever journey we choose. He provides actionable steps to give us clarity on the unique nature involved with leading winning teams."

—**Amobi Okugo,**
former professional soccer player turned
athlete entrepreneur and creator

"Trent's impact on our firm has been nothing short of transformative. With his guidance, our high-potential team and leaders have experienced significant growth, both personally and professionally. Through his insightful coaching, we've not only unlocked our team's potential but also propelled our firm forward year after year. *Leading Winning Teams* brilliantly captures the principles that Trent instilled in us, which contributed to our firm being a sought-after entity for acquisition. This book is a testament to his expertise and an invaluable resource for any organization aiming to achieve sustainable success."

—**Brian Sullivan,**
partner, Cherry Bekaert LLP (PKF Mueller)

"Trent's book is a game-changer for leaders at all levels. *Leading Winning Teams* provides strategies for achieving big league success. A must-read!"

—**Tom Coverly,**
TV show host, motivational speaker

"In *Leading Winning Teams*, Trent scientifically offers up the recipe of winning. A game-changer for anyone who seeks to be a leader in any industry."

—**Jamie Mittelman,**
founder and CEO, Flame Bearers

Who better to write *the* book on *Leading Winning Teams* than Trent Clark? (Three World Series rings is no leadership accident!) Trent understands how to help his readers blend the theory of winning with the reality of how to win. If you take leadership and winning seriously, and you're open to continuing to level up your ability and game, you *must* buy and read this book today!"

—**Mike Malatesta,**
CEO, best-selling author, and dream exit expert

"Wow! It's been a while since I've read a business book that really connects. The stories alone make this a page turner packed with so many lessons and insights."

—**Jeff Lem,**
founder and CEO, Portable Intelligence

"Winning doesn't happen by accident; it happens by design. Trent has captured that design perfectly in *Leading Winning Teams*. It is a must-read for those looking to win."

—**Phil Pelucha,**
founder, Billionaires in Boxers;
international award-winning usiness consultant

"I have known Trent for many years, and knowing him is to know the energy he puts into his craft. In his book *Leading Winning Teams*, you can feel his energy and his passion throughout! And that makes you want to read every page."

—**Dan Heuertz,**
CEO Hirize Inc

"Trent's first book is a powerful playbook, packed with actionable insights that elevate both personal growth and leadership."

—**Michael Levin,**
New York Times best-selling author

"As an entrepreneur who has shared the TEDx stage with Trent Clark, I can attest that *Leading Winning Teams* captures his game-changing strategies for sustainable excellence. This masterclass transcends sports, providing invaluable lessons in moral, mental, physical, and emotional conditioning to unlock any team's potential. With real-world insights woven throughout, Trent equips readers to set high standards, stay humble, and embrace continuous growth. Whether you're an executive or entrepreneur, the principles in these pages will inspire you and teach you how to assemble championship-caliber teams. I wholeheartedly recommend Trent's tour de force on achieving greatness."

—**Ethan King,**
best-selling author of *Wealth Beyond Money*;
co-founder of Zeus' Closet;
former president, Entrepreneurs' Organization (EO) Atlanta

"*Leading Winning Teams* is a transformative guide for anyone aspiring to elevate their leadership skills and cultivate high-performing teams. With practical strategies and insightful anecdotes, the author provides invaluable wisdom on fostering collaboration, inspiring motivation, and achieving collective success. This book is a must-read for leaders ready to unleash the full potential of their teams and drive impactful results."

—**Crystal Waltman,**
author of *Quitting to Win*

"Regardless of your experience, you can't help but learn from Trent and his teammates! There is wisdom in every chapter, and it comes alive with the stories shared!"

—**John Kassing,**
co-founder, Marquis Software

"Trent Clark has spent his professional life studying and teaching leadership. His messages on leadership in *Leading Winning Teams* will be valuable to any individual, young or old, who wants to become a better leader in any walk of life!"

—**Tim Selgo,**
Grand Valley State University Athletic Director (retired);
author of *Make One Play* and *The Anchor Way*

"Trent Clark is a passionate leader who always seeks to involve others in his work so we can all level up together. This is one of the characteristics that makes Trent stand out in the team building and leadership space. He is the leader who begins with serving and bringing others around a cause that improves the world. That's who I want to learn from and follow!"

—**Alex Sanfilippo,**
founder of PodMatch.com

"Trent Clark helped me get out of my own way. I had no comprehension of the unnecessary barriers I had been creating for my business, myself, and therefore invertedly for my family. Trent was crucial in guiding me through my business, which allowed me to change the direction and focus of the company. When I say I now know what my purpose in life is, it is important to understand that I am a United States Marine Corps Veteran where our life by design was to follow a purpose that disappeared like a magic trick when I left the service. Now, I truly understand what a purpose created by oneself means leading me to a purposeful, fulfilled, passionate, and happy lifestyle."

—Jeremy Spann,
Marine; entrepreneur; world-beater

"This book is a must-read for any leader looking to advance their team. *Leading Winning Teams* provides a blueprint for success through effective teamwork, motivation, and strategic planning. A game-winning read!"

—Ty Van Burkleo,
MLB coach and player (retired)

"I highly endorse *Leading Winning Teams* by Trent Clark. This book offers invaluable insights from a three-time World Series coach, translating elite sports strategies into real-world success. Through compelling stories and actionable advice, it teaches how to cultivate a team of high-performers, navigate adversity, and achieve extraordinary results. A must-read for anyone seeking to elevate their leadership and organizational prowess."

—Tanya Burnell,
vice president, Growth Equity and Sustainability,
Henry Crown and Company/CC Industries

A game-changer for leaders! *Leading Winning Teams* is a playbook for unlocking your team's full potential. A must-read for anyone serious about achieving big-league success.

—Dave Kerpen,
New York Times best-selling author of *Get Over Yourself:
How to Lead and Delegate Effectively for More Time,
More Freedom, and More Success*

Trent is the real deal. I met Trent through EO (Entrepreneurs' Organization), and this book reads just like having a conversation with him. In *Leading Winning Teams*, Trent brilliantly dissects the anatomy of success, revealing the winning combination of teamwork, motivation, and strategy. It is jam-packed with great takeaways—a masterpiece for leaders at all levels.

—Gail Davis,
Founder and president of GDA Speakers

LEADING

WINNING TEAMS

LEADING
WINNING TEAMS

HOW
TEAMWORK,
MOTIVATION,
AND **STRATEGY**
ACHIEVE
BIG LEAGUE SUCCESS

TRENT M. CLARK

WILEY

Library of Congress Cataloging-in-Publication Data:

Names: Clark, Trent, author.
Title: Leading winning teams : how teamwork, motivation, and strategy achieve big league success / Trent Clark.
Description: First edition. | Hoboken, New Jersey : Wiley, [2024] | Includes index.
Identifiers: LCCN 2024011119 (print) | LCCN 2024011120 (ebook) | ISBN 9781394247721 (hardback) | ISBN 9781394247745 (adobe pdf) | ISBN 9781394247738 (epub)
Subjects: LCSH: Teams in the workplace—Management. | Employee motivation. | Supervision of employees.
Classification: LCC HD66 .C4973 2024 (print) | LCC HD66 (ebook) | DDC 658.4/022—dc23/eng/20240315
LC record available at https://lccn.loc.gov/2024011119
LC ebook record available at https://lccn.loc.gov/2024011120

COVER DESIGN: PAUL MCCARTHY
COVER IMAGE: COURTESY OF THE AUTHOR, ANGELS BASEBALL LP
AUTHOR PHOTO: COURTESY OF THE AUTHOR

SKY10078623_070124

To my wonderful parents, I offer my deepest gratitude and respect. As I have traveled the world, I realize just how extremely fortunate and blessed I have been to have had you both in my life. My father was my coach, mentor, disciplinarian, advocate, and trusted advisor. We miss you every day, Papa. Your influence lives on through me every day. Mom, your unwavering support and mindset for abundance that you have passed on to us is incredible. You educated us that our only limitations are those we place on ourselves. Thank you for the unconditional love you provide and for believing in me always.

Contents

Acknowledgments

I WANT TO thank you for joining me on this journey, and I am excited to share all I have learned, as well as the stories and experiences of many other successful one-percenters. Below, are just some of the folks who have supported me during this process and have been a part of my journey in helping this project come to fruition.

First and foremost, I am thankful for Julie Kerr. As my editor and task expert, she has kept me and this project on track and assisted me throughout the process. She has poured herself into the text and takes my ideas, concepts, and strategies and creates value for the reader. I am grateful that she is on my team.

Also, I would like to thank the marketing team for this endeavor. Rachel Weaver, Nissa Jean Arellano, Michael Levin, and Vince Lanci have been instrumental in getting me prepared for the launch of this book and have added so much. Their ideas, dedication, experience, and brilliance astound me.

The guests of *Winners Find a Way* have been inspirational and key to the writing of this book, and each of them has contributed key elements to this project. You will find many of their quotes in this book, but many more have contributed to the theme and theories of our leadership and growth coaching.

The coaches who have shaped my abilities and learning on how to lead and mentor have been instrumental, along with the athletes I have coached. Special bonds are made along the way and I can think of so many, but here are some of the key influences in my life: Butch Perry, Tom Bommersbach, Darrell Davies, Joe Kruzel, Stan Sanders, Matt Eberflus, Pat Birney, Tim Selgo, Sparky Anderson, Brad Andress, Larry Herndon, Kirk Gibson, Alan Trammell, David Wells, Tom Izzo, Nick Saban, Ken Mannie, Gene Orlando, Tim Maxey, Fernando Montes, Brian Grapes, Mike Hargrove, Jim Thome, Kenny Lofton, Marquis Grissom, Paul DePodesta, Josh Byrnes, Manny Ramirez, Mark Shapiro, John Hart, Dan O'Dowd, Wendy Hoppel, Orel Hershiser, Joe Maddon, Mike Scioscia, Tim Mead, Matt Wise, Scot Shields, Tim Salmon, Mike Butcher, Scott Spiezio, Aaron Sele, David Eckstein, Shawn Wooten, Garrett Anderson, Jarred Washburn, John Lackey, Bud Black, Tony Reagins, Darrell Miller, Francisco Rodriguez, Don Wakamatsu, Ty Van Burkleo, Mike Couchee, Bobby Magallanes, Dino Ebel, Tim Buss, Arte Moreno, Dick Jacobs, and Bill Stoneman, as well as many more.

For the many days in baseball, I am forever grateful for some of that time talking business. My two passions of entrepreneurship and sports never wane. I stand in awe of Magic Johnson, a fellow Michigan kid, and a man I've known from a slight distance over the years from my days at Michigan State University, when we first met, to my work alongside of the Entrepreneurs' Organization (EO), where our paths crossed, with Magic educating me and my colleagues in his entrepreneurial learnings. In many ways, Magic has been an inspiration for athletes who have transitioned many of their skills as athletes to their skills in leading winning teams.

To my Wiley team, Christina Rudloff, Deborah Schindlar, Amy Handy, and Trinity Crompton: Thank you for the encouragement and support. I have learned so much and will continue to do so to do my best for your initiatives, as well as my own. Your guidance, patience, and leadership throughout this process has been instrumental—you are consummate professionals, and it is a pleasure to be your partner.

The leadership team at Bloom Growth make it happen every day. You are dedicated, smart, and savvy, and the organization is better for your involvement. To Todd Smart, your guidance is exceptional—the right leader. Isaiah, your unwavering support and real-world experience is impactful. Sheila Dodd, you've been so helpful and the key to keeping the train on the tracks. To Charlene, you make the whole thing go for us partners. No one moves forward without a little push from you, and the strength and energy you bring us with no reserve is uncanny and admirable. Every team needs a player like you on the team! Our partnership and process approach to growth allows each of us to scale. Thank you for challenging me every day and making us all better in the process.

To my wife, Kerri, for her unwavering support. I am thankful every day that we are on this life journey today and always. My children, Noah, Brig, Isaiah, Skylar, and Elijah—I take inspiration from each of you and I'm grateful to be your father. Just being a part of your growth as humans has been an inspiring journey that I never want to stop. I love you all, and you make everything I do better.

To the professionals and associates at *Winners Find a Way* podcast, Courage Coach, Athletic Influencer Marketing, and Leadershipity. Day in and day out, you make it happen for our clients. You help us set and maintain the standards for both us and the client and put them into practice. I stand in awe of your work ethic and your leadership, and am beyond thankful that you have chosen to share your time and talent with us. Thank you to Haley Toigo, David Gregory, Deepa Kartha, Joshua Conran, John Trainor, Rob Teis, Nissa Jean Arellano, and Luis Concha.

I have so many colleagues in my EO World who have had numerous hours alongside in forums, trainings, and global initiatives from the boards. I have learned so much. There are too many to mention, but the brief list is Jeremy Allen, Sid Bala, Dr. Amelia Case, Michael Hobbs, Jimi Michalscheck, Todd Gagerman, Michon Ellis, Ian Kieninger, Nancy Schumacher, Ryan Smallegan, Tim Volkema, Matt McKinney, Curtis Cottle, Tyler Cottle, Shannon Kasten, John Toigo, Joe Elias, Greg Gianino, Justin Bajema, Nick

Pope, Anthony Ramirez, Jeremy Spann, Jenny Feterovich, and many others.

I have been blessed with many mentors throughout my life. Don Hannah, a serial entrepreneur, YPO and WPO member, is one of those pivotal people who changed my life forever, as well as Peter Thomas, Scott Robinson, David Updegraff, Cary Chessick, Jerry Jenkins, my father, and some mentioned above.

Lastly, and certainly not least, to our clients: You put your trust in us every day. You have invited us into your boardrooms and your retreats, and allowed us to partner with you to realize incredible results and outcomes. You are the reason we exist. You provide us with the opportunity to do what we love, with people we admire.

If I have forgotten to mention anyone, it is certainly not intentional. I am fortunate to have a large group of supporters: friends, family, and colleagues who have encouraged me, helped me, challenged me, and influenced my thinking throughout this process.

Thank you, the reader, for proving that "leading winning teams" is as important to your team members and their families as it is to the strength and stability of your organization.

Trent M. Clark

Introduction

ONE OF THE most important lessons I have learned is that what you wish to accomplish cannot be done alone. Goals are important, but mentors are imperative. I would not have advanced without the many who came alongside to encourage me, reveal weaknesses, and train me in the skills needed to pursue my visions for the future. I am thankful to the many coaches who took their time to help me. And teams that win over and over and over again are relentless on process.

Choose: Acute Pain or Chronic Pain

There are two important types of pain in life: the pain of discipline and the pain of regret. You choose.

The Pain Exchange

It is October 24, 1995, game three of the World Series, Cleveland Indians versus the mighty Atlanta Braves. I am a 25-year-old Indians' coach in my second season in pro ball.

(continued)

1

(*continued*)

It is an extra-inning thriller, and our team is down two-zero in the Series. Then, in a near-midnight stroke of magic, veteran Eddie Murray steps up in the bottom of the 11th, a man built on consistent actions of discipline and preparedness, hitting the game-winning hit. *A triumph of great achievement!*

After being part of professional baseball, and over 2000 games, three World Series over 12-plus years, I learned a profound lesson—I call it the *pain exchange*. This lesson extends well beyond baseball; it resonates across elite forces, military, police, firefighters, artists, musicians, entrepreneurs, and world-class athletes. But the *pain exchange* is for everyone, everywhere, in everything you are looking to accomplish, a universal concept for all. The difference is that the above highlighted list goes into *deep training* from the best in the world and they know exactly what it takes.

Now, I'm *not* talking about the pain where your mom tells you to "stop being a pain in the neck" or when you get a little booboo on your finger. Not that pain!

I'm talking about the two pains in life: *the pain acquired through discipline, or the pain experienced with regret.* The question I pose is, which pain do you choose? The pain of discipline, a high value at a high cost but acute and short-lived pain? Or the pain of regret, a chronic pain that lingers for a lifetime?

Discipline is not always pleasant, but it produces a harvest of righteousness and peace for those trained by it. It is about acquiring treasures of learning the right way, satisfaction, and understanding through attained skills and wisdom.

Now, let us delve deeper into the essence of discipline. It is not just about enduring pain; it is a strategic choice. Consider the difference between acute and chronic pain. Acute pain, like the soreness after an intense workout, is short-lived. I am grateful for my health and being able to play with my grandkids on the floor and lift them up! Imagine 10 years from now lifting and playing with your grandkids, walking the golf course, taking a beautiful hike, waking up feeling healthy and well.

In my journey, discipline was the key. I have been through trials, learned from failures, and felt the acute pain of discipline in various forms, from bringing myself to nausea in hill running to pushing my physical and mental limits in business, travel, late-night meetings, and 4 a.m. workouts afterwards. But here is the thing about acute pain—it does not last. *It is a necessary part of growth, a short-term sacrifice for long-term gain.*

Winners understand this, embracing the acute pain to avoid the chronic pain of regret.

Now, let us consider the pain of regret—a chronic ache that replays in our minds. We have all faced moments where we were unprepared, unwilling to choose the harder but right path. Consider my state finals prep my senior year in high school—our baseball team's third state championship in a row. I'm resting on my laurels; I have a tweaked back from a muscle strain; I'm not doing my physical therapy and not as focused physically, mentally, and morally as I have been in the past and should be now. I will never have that chance again to go back. The state title is no longer an option—20 young boys with the biggest moment in our short lives, and the one we will remember for the rest of our lives—lost, but forever felt in the pain of regret.

The regret of our choices can endure for a lifetime. And we have all been there. My mother told me I shouldn't have gone to that party; the marital proposal, but the "one that got away"; my teacher told me I should study hard for this exam because the score could help me get into my dream school; my boss's

(*continued*)

(*continued*)

request to work diligently on this account as the next VP will be named by the participant's success.

In one of my early regrets, I recall letting my parents down as a boy, and then after being caught, taking up a lie about my disobedience to add kerosene to the current fire that was raging. That ended up in a wallop to my tushy, and though the physical punishment was an acute reminder, the disappointment in my parents' faces was what stayed with me. I had let them down. They probably questioned if I would be trustworthy in the future. I had crossed a line of our honesty—a stringent value in my household. That regret I carried for years.

As I transitioned from being an athlete to coaching world-class athletes, I observed a common trait among the most accomplished—self-discipline. It is a daily commitment to doing the hard things, meeting deadlines, learning continuously, and executing with precision. The best prioritize discipline over regret, knowing that, in the grand scheme of things, the acute pain of discipline is a small price to pay for satisfaction and wisdom.

Winners, in sports, business, or any field, understand this pain exchange. They also understand the importance of routines.

Consider the analogy of reviewing the tapes. Winners go back after the game and study the video. They analyze both what went wrong and, sometimes even more importantly, what went right! They make minor changes to those wrongs that yield a massive impact! It is a mindset of continuous improvement, a commitment to excellence.

Success is not just about being interested; it is about being committed to taking action every day. It is not about talking; it is about doing. Actions speak louder than words, and winners set themselves apart by their commitment to taking consistent action.

As we navigate our lives, we *constantly* encounter the pains of discipline and regret. Discipline should be the obvious choice. Understanding that acute pain is a stepping stone to triumph, embracing the daily grind, and accepting the challenges of difficult and strenuous routines gives you a major advantage. Most importantly, *discipline* is the first step to achieving your goals and consistently being successful.

To paraphrase Theodore Roosevelt, winners strive valiantly, knowing the triumph of great achievement. So my challenge to you today is this: in your daily choices, choose the pain of discipline, spend your energy on a worthy cause, and find your triumph of great achievement, just like Eddie Murray.

Are you ready to make the exchange?

Adapted from Coach Trent M. Clark's TEDx Talk in St. George, Utah, November 2023; Acknowledgment: Editors Jaime and Chris Lah

Make the *exchange*! You can do it. If you have never been trained to understand the benefits of discipline like world-class athletes have, that is okay. You can still conquer this, and we all have it inside of us. The decision to be disciplined is a choice you make moment by moment.

"Success is a choice"

– Rick Pitino

This book will include excerpts from over 30 interviews with prominent leaders as we discuss challenges in leading winning teams, and the many experiences that helped shape the ability to create our best possible team.

I have been a part of world champion teams, and others that needed a lot of improvement. My goal was to interview world-class leaders to stress-test my learnings from coaching with some of the best coaches in the world.

From Dave Fish, Head Coach (retired), Harvard Tennis (42 years); Head of Development, UTR Sports

Coaching is really about character development. It is about teaching people the art of self-improvement, to reach for excellence in all aspects of their life, and to take pride in the opportunity to meaningfully contribute to something that is greater than themselves.

Good coaches recognize the value of learning and contributing to the greater good of the community of which they are a part. They have mastered the ability to listen, learn, and be flexible in their approach to teaching while upholding strong moral values.

Sports and athletic programs teach young people responsibility: how to handle and manage stress, how to grow focus and discipline, and how to cultivate strong personal and professional values.

"If you're around excellence it's up to you to go out and participate in it and talk to people."

– Dave Fish

What is a coach? A coach can be defined as educator, listener, strategist, guide, mentor, confidant, friend, and authority, just to name a few.

Take Action

Each chapter includes quick **key takeaways** and an opportunity to put the readings into action in your *own* journey.

The concluding section of each chapter gives you the tools to do your own *pain exchange*. These present a pointed exercise to engage in so that you can get moving on your journey to leading winning teams.

Winners Find a Way

This experience of coaching the best in the world has created a constant solutions-minded view of attainment and production. There were challenges along the way and roadblocks too. This is where I really started to understand how critical it is for winners to find a way to win! I learned that I could overcome obstacles that were in my way and find solutions for obtaining my goals, or the end game. This has always been an adventure for me, and I have leaned into the challenges. I believe that I can face adversity and challenges successfully, because of many successes—along with too many failures to count—mentors, and experiences.

I have found that a lot of entrepreneurs are often the youngest in their family. As the youngest of four, I found immense value as a kid from the many times I got to see all the game films of my brothers and my sister going through repetitions in sports, music, school, and many other things. I also got to see my parents' reactions—both good and bad—to things that were happening in my siblings' lives. I was observant so I was taking in these action items and things that were happening in my brothers' and sister's lives. It helped me navigate my environment to gain efficiency, stay out of trouble, and please my parents (most of the time).

Incredibly early on, I learned that effort was extremely important. It was a variable I could control. I knew that if I practiced like I wanted to play, I would be ready for any game situation. I was that guy who wanted to be up to bat tied in the bottom of the ninth with two outs and the bases loaded. Combine effort with commitment and become a force to be reckoned with. Show me someone who exudes effort, and I will show you someone who has respect for both themselves and for the people they are serving whether that is their parents, their boss, their coach, their team, their opponents, their spouse, or their kids.

If You Measure It, You Manage It

Because I have had these great opportunities and experiences, I started a podcast a few years back called *Winners Find a Way*.

The show is based on a quote from *The Four Disciplines of Execution* that says, **"Winners, when shown data that they are losing, find a way to win."** That struck me immediately because that has been my entire life—scorekeeping on anything and everything, measuring marketing and sales statistics, wins and losses, scoreboards, and more measurements. Peter Lynch's famous quote, "What gets measured gets managed," reflects the importance of measurable goals. So I have been diligent about surrounding myself with winners who find a way to win! They are abundant-minded, solutions-driven people, willing not only to look at all options as a solution, but to commit strongly to the root cause of any challenge along the way so that they can find the process to resolve the challenge and meet their goals, repeatedly!

I joined the Entrepreneurs' Organization back in 2011. One of my mentors when I was 25 recommended that I join as soon as I could. The challenge with that is that only 3.4% of all North American businesses qualify for this exclusive organization. I was 41 when the fifth business I had started at that point qualified for the parameters to join the organization. This peer group has been transformative for my life and a testimony to the importance of surrounding myself with winners.

I learned along the way from good mentors in my family, and from friends and colleagues, to give back. I was given several gifts when I was born, strengths and attributes that other people may or may not have, and I feel obligated to share those strengths and fabulous experiences with others. I believe in passing along my good fortune to others who can benefit from these strengths that I have cultivated with the help of so many people.

1

Dreamer to Dream Maker

I WAS PROBABLY always seen as a dreamer. I certainly fit into the category of being a person who is a visionary.

When I was in seventh grade, I was in class with my favorite English teacher, Mr. Metcalf. He had decided that we were going to do "career week" at school, which included an assignment encompassing what life looks like when you're 30 years old. As a 12-year-old, I wasn't exactly focused on what life looks like at 30 but I knew that it was considered *really* old. After doing the math, I realized my 30th birthday would land on December 31, 1999. Although 1999 seemed another lifetime, its significance was heightened by Prince's then-current '80s hit "Party Like It's 1999."

First Written Goals Ever

I answered the five key questions Mr. Metcalf had asked us based on what I thought my career and life would look like when I was 30. The assignment I turned in probably looked like the ones from a bunch of other boys who also said they wanted to be a professional baseball player. My guess is that the teacher had a stack of papers that reflected similar big-time dreams. I certainly thought my goal was *really* big and I certainly thought it was *really* important.

I turned in that paper and never thought about it again. Or at least, that is how it seemed.

The Golden Ticket

Two years later, as a freshman in high school, I had an exceptionally good season in the spring. Summer baseball was starting, and I was again selected to an elite team that would compete for the state title in our age category, and likely the regional championships. One of the baseball camps near my home had an "invitation only" or combine-type camp (before those existed at the high school level) run by a former major league player and meant for the best of the best for the six to eight counties around the area. The invite felt like winning the golden ticket from *Willy Wonka*! Attending was something every aspiring baseball player longs for.

When the invite came in the mail, I was ecstatic. I was excited to play in front of a former major leaguer because I wanted to know if I had what it takes to make it. I noticed the invitation stated that if you were named the Most Valuable Player in this camp, you would have the opportunity to sit down with the director, the former major leaguer! When I read that, I was immediately motivated to do my absolute best so that I could ask him if he thought I had what it takes to make it.

Preparation Meets Opportunity

Even in high school, I knew what happens when preparation meets opportunity. I worked for the next four weeks on my hitting and my lifting, while continuing to practice and play with my summer team. I was training and preparing for this camp with a new level of intent and motivation that I had not put toward my baseball practice in the past.

Finally, camp week arrived. I had a fabulous week and was indeed named Most Valuable Player—a short-term goal accomplished!

I was ecstatic that I was going to get the chance to sit down with the director. Butterflies invaded my stomach for this decisive moment. I don't know if the director ever knew the weight this meeting would have for me. As I sat with him, I summoned the courage to mumble, "Do you think I have what it takes to be a major leaguer?" He paused for a moment, reiterating that he had a chance to see me all week and he was impressed. "I think you have what it takes." He believed that I could indeed make it at the major league level! I needed to hear those words from an expert.

Blind Courage

The next moment was one of those blind teenage dumb-courage moments that I probably would not have taken if I stopped to think about it. But I reached deep down beyond my fears, and I said to him, "With all due respect, everybody else is telling me no." The director again paused for a moment and asked, "Trent, who are all these people telling you no?" I responded, "My gym teacher, my freshman coach, my mom, my math teacher, and many others I've shared my goals with." Then he asked me, "Hey Trent, have any of these people that are telling you no ever played in the major leagues?"

I thought for a few moments, and it didn't take long to realize that none of them had actually played in the major leagues. I don't believe any of those folks had malicious intent or meant to squash my dreams, but they cared for me and simply wanted to keep me focused on the "backup plan" because it's a tough road to the major leagues and an infinitely small percentage actually make it.

My First Mentor Learning

The next thing the director told me was probably one of the most influential mentoring moments in my life that I still utilize today. He said, "Trent, I strongly caution you on where you take advice. If you are going to do something in this life, you should search out the people who have already *done it* and learn from them. I have done what you are looking to do, and I'm telling you that I believe you have what it takes."

I will never forget it. It was probably one of the biggest moments of my life to hear someone who had both authority and expertise tell me exactly what I wanted, and likely needed, to hear. My inner voice was telling me no and reiterating the points of all the people who had told me no. I was telling myself, "You're not strong enough, you're not fast enough, you're not big enough . . . you are *not* enough."

Don't "Should" on Me

All my self-talk changed the day this person told me I had what it takes. I have followed his advice ever since that moment. I learned that if I'm going to ask people for advice, I need to have qualified them on their experience before I ask them for it. This is the challenge when people offer their opinions and advice without being asked for it and without having expertise on the subject in question. The moment people start "shoulding" on me ("You should do this . . . you should do that"), my mind immediately races to whether they are an authority and have the relevant experience for me to listen to opinions from them.

I took that advice and gained great confidence not only in the belief of what I could do but continual study into being the best version of myself. That started with following what my inner voice was telling me. I started looking at sports psychologists like Jim Loehr, who would speak and write on how important it is for athletes to monitor their self-talk. I became entrenched in the children's book *The Little Engine That Could*. I knew that I had to be telling myself, "I believed in me" just as much as I needed reinforcement that others believed in me, and probably even more.

"I think I can, I think I can, I think I can."

– The Little Engine That Could

I gained a lot of confidence with my positive self-talk and I also started garnering increased success. I certainly was attributing the success in my schooling, my sports performance, and anything else that was important to me to positive mental imaging and positive self-talk. I was utilizing the techniques in choir, glee club, and other areas of my life. The results proved to have terrific value both for the advice itself and for the work I was willing to do to position myself for success and stay positive in demanding situations, often under duress.

Dream Maker

As I continued these skills through my college days at the Division I level at the University of Toledo, I was increasingly injured due to the continuous strains I was placing on my body. So as a 23-year-old with a pretty beat-up body and a torn rotator cuff, I was told that my dream of being a professional baseball player was likely over. The only way to continue my dream of being in the major leagues would be as a coach, and I was told I should transition to that career in professional baseball . . . now! That was a difficult thing to hear, but I was ready for that discussion because I was physically, mentally, and morally drained from trying to heal from injury and fatigued from the day-in, day-out stresses of looking to overcome these injuries to compete with the best in the world. I knew I was already giving up a sizeable physical advantage being a five-foot-six-inch, 170-pound player.

I made that switch and transitioned from *dreamer to dream maker*. I focused my efforts on all that I had learned and studied in education, exercise physiology, and strength and conditioning to create value for other players on their journeys.

As a 25-year-old coach, I entered the 1995 World Series with the Cleveland Indians. I achieved my dream that had begun 15 years earlier when I was running around my backyard hitting wiffle balls over the fence, picturing myself in game seven of the World Series. Standing in the dugout in 1995, I looked out on the field watching 50 or 60 men living out the dream. I was a part of it! It was an incredible experience to have accomplished something so rare, something I had been dreaming about my whole life.

A Letter from School

In December 1999, I traveled from Arizona, where I was living, to Michigan for the holidays. I had not seen my parents very much so I was excited to get home. My wife and I would celebrate our son's first Christmas experience at one and a half years old, as well as my sister's 32nd and my 30th birthday. Being from Michigan, I really appreciated a white Christmas.

When I arrived home my mother said, "Mail came for you from the school." I assumed that was a fundraising letter from my college. But it was from the grade school, and when I opened it I saw my assignment from Mr. Metcalf. In a quick hand-written note, he wrote, "How did you do?" I really hadn't thought about that assignment since turning it in all those years ago, but I was suddenly transported back to that moment of being a 12-year-old and I was ecstatic just remembering the excitement of how important that assignment was to me then. There in that envelope were my answers to those five questions he had asked us to consider in 1982—18 years earlier.

The first question he asked us to consider was "What will I be doing after high school?" My answer: *I would be attending Arizona State University where I would be playing baseball.* I did not attend ASU, but I did play both tennis and baseball in college at the University of Toledo.

The second question was the all-encompassing "What will I be doing for a career when I'm 30 years old?" My answer: *I will be playing professional baseball in the major leagues.* I never made it as a player, but I was in my sixth year coaching, now for the Los Angeles Angels, and I had coached in two World Series!

The third question was "Where will I be living and be working?" My answer: *I will be living in a golf and tennis community in Arizona.* I was focused on leaving the Midwest and getting out of the cold winters that I had known for my first 12 years, and I did not see myself experiencing any more than 18 years of them. And now I had just flown in the night before from our golf and tennis community home in Mesa, Arizona!

The fourth question was "What will my personal life look like?" My answer: *I will be married to a blonde girl taller than me!* That was not that hard at five-foot-six but I did do that, and I have been married to her now for 29 years, and we have five children together, and a grandson.

The final question was "What will my family look like?" My answer: *My wife and I will have a son.* That day, reading my answers, our son, Noah, was a year and a half.

The Results

This seventh-grade assignment was my first exercise in goal setting and vision work on what the future might look like, and the experience of writing out my goals. I never assumed that these goals would be so influential in my life, but the impact was clear. Putting my goals on paper had been paramount in my success. I believe it is one of the reasons I stayed so focused on what I genuinely wanted to become and how and where I would live and engage in this world. It not only shaped my decisions about the people I spent time with and those who would help me meet the expectations and goals I had placed upon myself, but also helped me eliminate relationships in my life that might possibly keep me from achieving those goals.

Hyper-Learning and Adaptability
Cory Proctor, NFL Player, Dallas Cowboys

Cory is an unlikely NFL offensive lineman from the U of M—no, not Michigan, but the University of Montana. His rise to stardom was based on grit, having the physical size required, and being able to learn quickly.

Today, Cory is helping other athletes plan their future after the game through his wealth management firm. He has a special bond with his clients, having played in the NFL himself.

(continued)

(*continued*)

Cory's superpower is adaptability—the willingness to be prepared for the things that are unlikely to happen, in addition to being fundamentally sound in what is expected too.

When Cory joined me on *Winners Find a Way*, I was excited to uncover his journeys both to pro sports and to entrepreneurship.

TRENT: WHAT WAS THE BIGGEST MOTIVATOR FOR YOU TO DRIVE CONTINUOUS IMPROVEMENT FOR BOTH YOUR PRO SPORTS CAREER AS WELL BEYOND THAT TOO?

Cory: You go through the seasons of what drives you, and what brings you division transforms at different times.

When I got into football, what drove me honestly was praise from my coach. And when I started in seventh grade, I was going through some turmoil with my folks' divorce. And it's just what it is. I'm not talking bad about them. They loved us. They loved me and my brothers like crazy. But it was a hard time for them. So they handled it as best as they could and so walking through that is still confusing and weird and was an emotional time for where I was a kid—8, 9, 10, 11 years old. And so when I got into seventh grade, we moved around a bunch, and I found football. The first time I remember we were doing Oklahoma drill, and a coach just needed a running back. So he yelled at me to get in there. And I'm just a pudgy kid holding the football, and I don't know why. But for whatever reason, I just decided to go really hard and put in a big effort on that play. And I was just a kid learning how to work on the field and didn't even play football, but I just decided to go hard and try to hit the guy. Well, I bowled them all over. I hit the linebacker in the Oklahoma drill, bowled him over, and coach flipped out on me like yelling and screaming all excited because

I just laid him out head on. And that just threw an explosion of endorphins into my head. My receptors were just going crazy! And all of a sudden, I was like "Whoa, I've got all this praise from somebody, for doing something good!" I wanted more of that. "Go ahead, keep going, that's great"—that reinforcement was that initial driver for me in a big way. Positive reinforcement. I wanted that praise from my coaches.

DID THAT CHANGE YOUR BEHAVIOR? AND WERE YOU SUDDENLY GETTING THE RESULTS THAT YOU HADN'T OTHERWISE?

If the coach told me to be somewhere I'm going to be there. I became extremely coachable with all coaches. I loved to bust my butt and was willing to go kill myself for somebody, almost to a fault. And then over the years it shifted. Then I had this conditioning work ethic that I got from that, which was a really big deal. Then I operated on this conditioning and a little skill. But then it started shifting over, especially when I got my faith, to have confidence in knowing that I was set apart from the average person in this world.

ALL THESE THINGS YOU WERE LEARNING ON THE FIELD OF PRIORITIZATION AND STUDYING THE GAME, WHAT WAS IT THAT YOU LEARNED THAT HELPED YOU BECOME THE LEADER OUTSIDE OF SPORTS?

I love asking averages. So when I got into the financial business, I was like, what's the average amount of study time to get licensed, and what's the average income level of an advisor? And what's the average revenue for assets under management for a typical financial firm? When I started my own firm, I asked myself, "What are these averages I need to make?"

(continued)

(*continued*)

YOU ARE NOW A TRAINED HYPER-LEARNER AND ADAPTABLE BEYOND THE NORMAL HUMAN SCOPE. AND BECAUSE YOU ARE A MASSIVE OVERACHIEVER, WHY DID YOU CARE SO MUCH ABOUT THE AVERAGES?

Why do I ask about the average? Because average is pretty weak in this world, and I know I can get the average—I will smash that.

And so, whatever it is, and it does not matter if I don't know what the field is, because that's just a language. I just have to learn it. I have an ability to learn, especially in the league, when you have to interview with these teams, or they want to get you down, when you're picked up on a football team in the NFL, you have to know the offense. The coach will come in individually in a meeting, and he will drop down two or three plays. And you have to know all the calls, and everything that's going on with the players. If you don't, he will retest you the next day. And if you don't know 90-plus percent of those calls—basically ace the test—you're gone, you're cut.

I knew I could go after it. So that was what separated me in a big way from the rest of the world. When I was operating through something I was learning, I knew that my competence gave me a whole different level of work learning.

WHAT WAS THE BEST LEARNING ABOUT THE SKILLS AND SUPER-POWERS YOU WOULD USE TO MOVE FROM NFL STAR TO BUSINESS LEADER?

Because the kind of superpower that goes with sport is realizing that your own strength is you have to have vision, but realizing your vision is finite. If I can make that vision a reality and if I can find the right people to give me the right information, to go carry through the right tasks, and not waste a ton of my time, then I will get to my destination—from point A to point B—10 times faster than I ever would have trying to do it myself.

PRO ATHLETES AND HIGH-PERFORMING ACHIEVERS BATTLE BETWEEN CONFIDENCE VERSUS ARROGANCE?

What it does for one's confidence, but I don't want people to get that mixed up with cockiness either, right? Arrogance! Because I can be confident that I know I can get it done. But don't be arrogant, believing that you know everything. And you're probably in the same boat—the more I find out, the more I weaponize myself. And the more I realize that I don't know it all.

Now you have to walk through the bad times, but most people are trying to pour from an empty cup without confidence.

What I love sharing with guys is we're conditioned with an ability to learn and transition; the normal person is not. And everybody has that ability, but we're conditioned to it! I have a level of learning that I can attain information way higher than the norm.

– Cory Proctor

The Two Transferables

As top athletes transition from their many years of training to be the best they can be at sport, they bring *all* their education and learnings and apply it to other leadership roles and likely a new career. The first of the two transferable superpowers that separate top athletes is the fact that they are hyper-learners—they have an ability to learn skills and strategies very quickly and are prepared to act on those learnings very quickly. They are action driven.

The second is their ability to adapt very quickly and still exe-cute on an extremely elevated level. The most notable success measure for athletes is often based on executing under pressure and duress. Because athletes flex these mental, emotional, and physical muscles all the time, they have great confidence in their ability to overcome a situation and still come out ahead of their competition. The best in the world are fabulous at this.

I Hire Athletes

Jim Ayres, President, Amway North America (retired);
Former College Football Player

As the retired president of Amway North America, Jim Ayers has had experience with thousands of employees. As a former athlete himself, he understands that athletes love feedback and are conditioned and trained for continuous improvement. Some of the other key features of athletes that teams and organizations love are coachability, and being results-driven, solutions-minded, and competitive, along with being physi-cally and mentally strong.

A good friend introduced Jim to me because he is such a process-oriented guy, and loves to support his alma mater, Grand Valley State University. He talks openly about not having focus and direction as a kid and being a bit lost in his teen years. It was his football coaches who gave him purpose and helped him understand how to be a contributor to a team.

Jim climbed a ladder in one of the most esteemed family businesses in the country—Amway. He was fortunate to have many talented players around him, and he worked diligently to select the right players for his Amway work team.

Jim joined me as a guest on *Winners Find a Way*.

TRENT: YOU HAVE HAD A GREAT RUN OF HIRING FABULOUS
TEAM MEMBERS AND DEVELOPING YOUR TEAMS IN YOUR
BUSINESS CAREER. IS THERE A "SECRET SAUCE" YOU CAN
LET US IN ON?

Jim: When I was in any of my positions, but especially leading a big company, when I'm trying to hire somebody for any
position, I'm looking for technical ability, for knowledge, all
that stuff. But what I'm really looking for is that want, and
desire. That is an example for others, because that's the way
you are. And I talked about this a little in the past but it's
not a "make-or-break" thing. If I've got three or four very
equal candidates for a position, if one of them was a captain
of her high school volleyball team or something, I'm going
for that person. Probably because she has been through the
crucible of challenge and all the challenges that come with
athletics. I don't care what level it is you are playing at; it
teaches you.

WHAT WAS ONE OF THE BIGGEST SKILLS YOU LEARNED FROM
SPORT THAT REMAINS A STAPLE IN YOUR LIBRARY OF LEARNING
THAT YOU HAVE APPLIED TO YOUR BUSINESS CAREER?

Visualize coming events and prepare for them. That is how you
are at your best when the time comes.

WHAT DID YOU LEARN FROM RISKING IN SPORT THAT WAS
ULTRA-HELPFUL IN YOUR CAREER?

I always looked for opportunities that were big, scary, and
impactful that a lot of people didn't want to tackle. And I
would be like, raise my hand, sign me up, man. I'm going to
make that happen. And that was a big thing for me. In fact,

(continued)

(*continued*)

that's one of the habits, and I'm really big into the habits for success.

One of the habits that I work on all the time, in my career and in my life, when I'm faced with something that scares me and that makes my stomach turn, my human instinct is I want to step back from that, and I try to make it a habit, when I feel that way, to recognize it and step towards it. And every bit in my career, every big opportunity that I had that scared the heck out of me, and I wasn't sure, or I did not know if I could do it, but I made myself step towards it, not away from it. And I tell you, that always worked out for me. It made me better, just like back to the football drills in college. If you asked me about fundamental habits for success, that is one that I recommend to everybody.

WHEN SPEAKING ON THE HABITS OF SUCCESS, WHAT ARE THE BIG ITEMS LEADERS MUST GET RIGHT BOTH PHILOSOPHICALLY AND BEHAVIORALLY?

My leadership philosophy is three simple things: confront reality, speak the truth, and there is never a wrong time to do the right thing. That's it.

I've got five leadership behaviors under that:

1. I think about how I want to behave every day, in every interaction I have.

2. Humility. I do not have the answers. I need people. It is transparency. I tell you the truth 100% of the time, no exceptions, no BS, full transparency.

3. I meet commitments. When I say I'm ready to do something, I do it, and it builds trust.

4. I give credit and take blame. Always give credit and take blame as a leader, 100% of the time.
5. I serve others. I'm here to help you be successful; it is not about me.

Those are the principles that I get back to daily.

"Visualize coming events. Prepare for them. That is how you are at your best when the time comes."

— *Jim Ayres*

Key Takeaways

- Put your dreams and aspirations into writing.
- Be prepared when opportunities arise.
- Achieving small goals builds momentum for larger ones.
- Hyper-learning is a key to success.
- Skills gained through sports are transferable to other ventures.
- The impact of mentorship on personal and professional growth cannot be overstated.

The Pain Exchange

Identify three winning mentors/peers to surround yourself with and plan for how you will find a way to win.

1. First Person: Make a list of the five most influential people you know of who have already accomplished what you are looking to do. Prioritize this list from one to five. Go big on this. If you want to be the best investor in the world, then Warren Buffet may be the top of your list. Ask! All that the person can say is no. You will be *shocked* at how infrequently the most brilliant minds are asked to help someone. *Goal: Upskill mentally, physically, and morally.*

- Key items: Be persistent to get an answer and have a value proposition. What will you offer them? Limit your exposure to one hour per month to start (they likely will go over time). Make those meetings so dynamic with goals, plans, and preparation that they love the rapid-fire intensity. Lean into this approach, not away from it.
- Stay aligned: You want to find a person who has similar values as you.
- Go down your list: If number one says no, thank them, ask them for a referral to someone they know who is as good as they are and may be willing. This will not only get their wheels turning, but their ego may not allow them to refer someone else and they may take the deal! If the no is final, get number two on the phone asap. If it's no again, hit up number three asap. You likely won't get to number five.

2. Second Person: Physical training partner. *Goal: Physical and mental conditioning.*
   - This can be a personal trainer, a workout partner, or a committed exercise group experience.
   - Set your number of workouts per week, times, exercises/plan, place, communication strategy, and a one-month reward you will plan *together*.
   - Set your goals and celebrate together *every month* (unless you falter). Be diligent and make the reward worth it. Stretch yourself on this and then commit to it. If the juice (reward) is worth the squeeze (discipline/execution) and it aligns with your best self, you will win!

3. Third Person: Spiritual mentor. *Goal: Moral conditioning.*
   - This will seem like the easiest person to find, but don't let it be. Be rigorous and set the highest standards here for yourself. (Note that this may be a person you pay, such as a top author in a discipline, or a counselor.)

- This list should be made in the same way you made your list of five influential people, but take extra time to make this list and assure you have admiration and respect for this person, and it will remain throughout the experience. You may not agree with each thing this person asks of you, but alignment here must be at another level; being equally yoked in this relationship is important.

A note of caution: Like you, all these folks are fellow humans. Because they are human, they may let you down, disappoint you, and fail your expectations. If you lay out your expectations of the relationship to start, this is less likely to happen, and be clear on what your mentors and peers can expect from you. You may let them down, but winners do not do this frequently, so commit to making it right, and to winning!

"What one man can do, so can another."

– Sir Anthony Hopkins in *The Edge*

Protect this time and these sessions as if it is life or death. We are all getting better or worse every day; there is no in-between. These meetings will help direct your steps on the daily until your next meeting to assure you are moving to be better every day.

2

Lessons That Transcend Sports

The Underdog Story

I love the overachiever story, or the story of the underdog. They are never boring. So it always bothers me when people say, "Baseball is so boring!" For the novice who does not know most of the rules and the strategy of the game, it may look like there are a lot of people standing around for a long time. There appears to be little activity between short bouts of action. Over the years people have decided baseball is "slow" and there is a general misunderstanding of baseball's intensity. What is happening is mental and strategic warfare—there is always great intensity.

One of the major challenges in baseball is hitting—being a batter. This is often considered one of the most difficult skills of all athletic endeavors and is therefore rewarded handsomely when someone is successful 30% of the time.

A batter steps into the batter's box for what appears to be a game of one-on-one. But the pitcher invites eight of his closest friends to help reduce the risk, or eliminate the threat of the batter reaching base, by strategically coming behind him, and the batter (catcher) covering up most of the exposed areas inside the boundaries where the batter might hit the ball. The batter is scouted, and the team works in tandem through their alignment to eliminate the threat to the best of their ability. It becomes a one-versus-nine scenario and the odds become increasingly poor for the batter.

The other significant challenge is that the batter has no idea what pitch is coming. The pitcher controls the speed, angle, spin, and placement of the ball to reduce the threat or risk of the batter striking it hard, and far. Thus I root for the little guy who stands at the plate facing all the odds and who must overcome all factors to have a sliver of success. Thus, baseball is really a modern-day David and Goliath story!

Like David, the batter must be in strict training and have experience to be successful on this field of battle. While most people recognize David from the biblical story, what they may not know is that David—though just a young shepherd—had great strength with God on his side. First, he had worked in the fields for many years and was charged with protecting his father's assets, his flock of sheep. David went to great lengths to protect that flock by slaying both a bear and a lion. While he was small, he clearly was mighty, skilled, and thoughtful to eliminate a threat that was much greater in size, strength, and speed.

The big lesson in baseball is in a batter's perseverance, ability to adjust, return to the battle, and try to win despite a much greater percentage of losses. Strength develops in facing adversity, learning to overcome, and becoming resolute. Kids who have grown up in baseball and played at a highly competitive level throughout high school, or beyond, are conditioned to face adversity, strategize, adapt, learn continuous improvement, and find a way to be successful under strenuous conditions that they cannot control.

If you described an employee as someone who faces adversity, strategizes, adapts, learns, continually improves, and finds a way to be successful under challenging conditions, I would certainly want that person on my team!

Lessons That Transcend Sports
Desmond Clark, NFL Player; Entrepreneur; Speaker

I first met Desmond "Dez" Clark when we were on a speaking docket at the famed Metropolitan Club in the Willis Tower in Chicago. His spirit of faith, football, and a passion for discipline was a huge attraction for me and we hit it off.

Dez has run both an insurance group and now a transportation and logistics group. He has welcomed change and challenges in his life, rising to each and taking them head on.

Dez was one of our first interviews on *Winners Find a Way*, and he never disappoints (and he does a lot of public speaking too—call him!). We talked about some of our coaches along the way and some great instructors who taught us many things.

TRENT: WHAT WAS ONE OF THE DRIVING TAKEAWAYS FROM LEARNINGS ON BEING YOUR BEST AND HAVING SUCH CONSISTENCY THROUGHOUT YOUR CAREER?

Dez: Anything that you do should be "how" you do everything, which means your standard is your standard. You do not lower your standard over here and then raise your standard over there; your standards should be the same no matter if you are talking to someone on the streets or talking to the president. It is about how you work when no one is looking or how you work out with your teammates. You should have the same standard all the time.

(*continued*)

(*continued*)

MANY PEOPLE THINK MODERN-DAY ATHLETES ARE GETTING "SOFT" AND CODDLED TOO MUCH. HOW DID YOU GET AND CONTINUE TO KEEP YOUR INNER DRIVE?

Always choose your standards over your feelings. If you want to be in the 1%, if you want to sustain a certain level of success and be able to maintain it, it does not matter who is watching you. You know if you are putting in the work.

GIVE US A GLIMPSE INTO YOUR INNER DRIVE, AND HOW THAT SHOWS UP EVEN AFTER A PRO FOOTBALL CAREER.

I work out with my daughter in the morning, and somebody in that class hit 100% output. Because you are on the heart monitor for accuracy, I was like, who hit 100%!? So I dropped my daughter off at school, and I always go back for a second workout, because I want to hit 100%. I haven't done it yet. I go in and I'm working, I'm doing the boxing, I'm doing jumps and everything, and I get up to 92 . . . 93 . . . 94, and then I get up to 96, but I was like ah, oh, hey! Then I started thinking to myself, "Man, you are a little sick. You are in here by yourself, and it doesn't matter who saw it." It was between me and myself. I was pushing the hardest to hit that 100%. I was not trying to prove it to anybody but myself.

> "Your standard is your standard. You do not lower your standard. You should have the same standard all the time. Always choose your standards over your feelings."
>
> – Desmond Clark

As Desmond says, if you must lower your standards to be a part of an organization, because you are looked at as too aggressive or as a teacher's pet because your achievements are above the standard, it may be time to go to another organization. It's probably a good indication that the way you value hard work and effort is not being met with the same vigor.

I have seen many people raise the standard of an organization, and the organization resets to that standard, and then resets that standard for team members.

At the end of the day, what Dez is really talking about is how it is important for you to feel your work has an impact and about the contribution you are making. The standards are set and can be measured.

The lessons we can learn from sports transcend nearly everything we do. One of the greatest awards given in sports is for sportsmanship. It recognizes the person who is poised under pressure, maximizes focused effort, honors their teammates, demonstrates respect to the opposing team, and maintains an attitude of positivity while carrying themselves with dignity. Again, if you tell me I'm onboarding an employee with these qualities, I'm thinking we hit a home run to have such a person work alongside us.

Trained in Adversity and Failure

As young athletes go through the trials and tribulations of sport, a huge advantage is gained as they learn and are conditioned through practice, training, coaching, and countless hours of repetition to deal with adversity and failure. This may be the most important quality and skill learned from the power of sport.

Life is going to deal us blows, and we'll be left with challenges that we'll have to face. Those experiences from sport will seem more insignificant compared to the adversity we face in our relationships, our jobs, careers, and even the adversity we face in life and death. But it gives us fortitude and the confidence to take on challenges because we have been trained in those skill sets through sport.

I do believe that overcoming adversity is a learned skill. Athletes become experts at this through having to overcome numerous obstacles and challenges. These little lessons give us repetition and create confidence in our ability to overcome the various challenges in our own lives.

Read, Read the Bible

One consistent principle of discipline has been an element of walking by faith. And that includes taking time daily to reflect in the word of a higher power. First, I think it keeps players humble. When talking about eternity, ethics, and faith, it is easy to see that the greater good of this entire world is not mired in sports.

Second, I like the statement "There is no wrong way to do the right thing." For athletes who are physically and mentally conditioned, that is an incredible head start in being the best you can be. But if you are not spending time morally conditioning, I think that is an error and may be your downfall. Pride comes before the fall.

Our journey in sports should translate to knowing the right thing, being able to *do it,* and modeling that behavior for others, then leading the journey with teams in the future on clear conduct expectations of our shared values as an organization. Reading inspiring books and studying authors of wisdom and ethics helps us develop the ability and consciousness to act in kindness, respect, wisdom, and integrity.

If our leaders always modeled these behaviors, most of us would enjoy work more, teams would be more productive, and it would help each of us grow as brothers, sisters, friends, leaders, fathers, mothers, spouses, and as grandparents. We are back to this game, these sports, these small dichotomies of life—how do we want to show up in challenging situations? It starts with learning what it takes to stay focused on the things that matter, and not getting caught up in the things that are less of a priority.

An inferior performance is a direct shot to our confidence. Grace is vital for our mental health and moral conditioning. If we do not extend that grace to ourselves, the negative self-talk starts, and you are literally sapping your own confidence from your body.

Confidence Equals Prep and Reps

Preparation plus repetition equals confidence. When we are well prepared, we feel better about our opportunities, and we have confidence. Then when facing any new skill set for the first time, we have a built-in mechanism to keep us safe. We are cautious and often that is not a terrible thing. The idea that we take things slow is wise and allows us to adapt and become accustomed to something new. I use driving as an example in a section later in this chapter ("Confidence for Young Drivers") to discuss the very element of how we gain great confidence over time—after we are well prepared and have had significant numbers of repetitions.

Confidence versus Arrogance

Confidence is necessary to achieve success. Without it you can hardly continue to compete with the best in the world, who also have self-confidence. The challenge is recognizing the difference between confidence and arrogance. The difference usually comes down to a lack of humility.

The division between confidence and arrogance can be a gray area. The first thing I listen for is a change in language from "we" to "me," "us" to "them," and too many uses of "I" in any sentence.

The sentence "I don't know if you know, but I'm kind of a big deal" is commonly offered as a joke, often after a major slight to the ego or a huge slice of "humble pie." The utterance helps any top performer level themselves; while it is fabulous to be admired for a certain skill, we are all humans with God-given skills that are our superpowers. And we're all different and will choose which skills we want to develop. I think it is a subtle reminder to "stop believing your press clippings."

"Proper preparation prevents poor performance."

– John Wooden

The Five Ps

The key element of this is "proper." I see teams and organizations working diligently with a full commitment from team members, yet it may not be prioritized properly. Basketball coach John Wooden was renowned for entertaining fellow coaches. And you may be thinking they were coming to see the mighty UCLA Bruins play against a worthy opponent. Wrong! They came to watch practice. Coach Wooden established exactly what "proper" was in this world: two hours each day of undivided attention, never late, value the time, and be mentally and physically ready to do your best and improve.

I am sure the UCLA players were frustrated that Coach Wooden was a time-hawk and expected his players to learn the value of it. I'll value your time and you'll value mine was his clear message. Mutual respect was his standard.

Confidence for Young Drivers

Take the example of driving a car as an indicator of how prep and reps play out in our modern-day society. Getting a driver's license entails many hours of classroom time and study, along with over 25 hours or more (depending on which state you live in) of driving with a licensed adult driver. Plus there are required hours alongside a specialty driving instructor with experience teaching basic mechanics and driving techniques like parallel parking and merging on to the interstate, among other skills.

There is a test of the study materials on operating, safety, rules, and more, and then a skilled driving examination must be completed to attain the license. I recall it being an extremely nerve-racking process. As the youngest of four kids, I had already seen my siblings go through this strict training to gain this priceless award that really breached a hurdle from being a child into adulthood—and freedom. Most adolescents who receive this license have extraordinarily little confidence in their ability, and they take an overly cautious approach to this great responsibility. It makes perfect sense because they have had some preparation but extraordinarily little repetition—more time is required studying the rules of driving than actually doing it.

Most of us don't think about the great responsibility we undertake each time we get behind the wheel because we've been doing it for a while. I have an ultra-level of confidence due to my nearly 40 years of driving experience. The amount of repetition has allowed me a near unconscious level of confidence in monitoring countless mechanisms in my car: temperature, radio controls, cruise control, mirror adjustments, tire pressure gauges, and countless others, all while looking outward to be aware of traffic signals, boundary lanes, signage, and potential hazards, as well as distractions like billboards and the landscape that catches the eye. There are probably over 50 things my brain is filtering while I'm driving, and I do it nearly unconsciously now. If my wife asks me to drive to the store to get a loaf of bread, I don't have to ask myself, "Where does the key go? How do I start the car? Which one is the brake, and which one is the accelerator?" None of those things even enter my mind because I do them unconsciously.

Expertise is like that. We gain a level of confidence due to our countless hours of preparation and repetition. Athletes undergo this strict training to hone their skills to be successful in their sport. And when they leave that sport, they have become hyper-learners knowing the great advantage of focusing on learned skills by being given proper preparation and the repetitions necessary to advance that skill. This concept is ingrained as continuous improvement and can make athletes fabulous employees who can be shaped and directed to learn these skills to provide remarkable success for an organization.

Be Great Right Where You Are

David Morehouse, President, Pittsburgh Penguins (retired); President Clinton's Forward Man; Boilermaker

David was likely the most magical interview I have ever had in my life, and I have done hundreds of them. At the time of the interview, David was the president of the Pittsburgh Penguins. I will never forget how gracious he was with his time.

(continued)

(*continued*)

I happened to be on a speaking docket at NYU Shanghai. The interview had been scheduled long before my travel plans were solidified, so I was not going to consider changing it. The interview was scheduled for 1 a.m. local time in Shanghai and I probably sound drunk on the recordings because of my fatigue levels, but I was entranced from the beginning because David is a dynamic person. We spoke for over two hours and I was so jazzed up that I was ready to run across the city at 3:30 in the morning!

What most people do not know about David is that his journey to the presidency of a major sports team was far from "standard." He was never a pro hockey player or even any type of professional athlete. He was a boilermaker from Pittsburgh who wears his associate degree from Allegheny Community College as a badge of honor.

Once David had a chosen professional skill, he tested his skills in bigger arenas with the Democratic Party, and within local politics. He moved quickly, showing that his skills could have valuable impact, and becoming a forward person for the White House and President Clinton.

TRENT: INEXPERIENCE ON THE JOB IS OFTEN LOOKED AS "LESS THAN"—LESS VALUE AS A CONTRIBUTOR, OR BEING THE FNG (THE FRIGGIN' NEW GUY/GAL). YOU HAVE A DIFFERENT LENS ON THAT. PLEASE EXPLAIN.

David: Not knowing everything or how to fully operate in a new role is not a weakness. You learn as you go and often those who don't know everything offer a unique perspective—one outside the box.

WE OFTEN TALK ABOUT LEARNING MORE FROM THE LOSSES THAN THE WINS. WHAT HAS BEEN YOUR EXPERIENCE?

You can learn a lot more from losing than succeeding, and then moving past those mistakes you have made and keep going. Keep working hard.

YOU HAVE REINVENTED YOURSELF REPEATEDLY THROUGH NEW OPPORTUNITIES. WHY DO YOU THINK THEY KEPT TAPPING YOU ON THE SHOULDER FOR MORE?

You never know where you will end up or where life will take you. Perseverance and hard work can take you far. I always strived to be the best at whatever I was doing at the time. I recall thinking, "I could never do things my superiors could do," when I started with an organization, but after a year I had developed skills that made me believe that I likely *could* one day get to those skills. And I was often chosen to replace my boss when they had moved on because of my continuous learning and commitment to being the best I could be.

"You cannot play great every day, but you can play your hardest every day"

— David Morehouse

Only Judged on the Role You're in Now

As athletes progress, one of the things they learn is that there are roles they'll take on to help their team. Each role is distinct and comes with different expectations and responsibilities. Athletes often want to play the game in a different and bigger role than they currently have, a role where they feel they would be better and have more impact on the game and for their team. Inexperienced players often get placed in smaller roles to prove that they could manage a larger role after they have gained more experience and wisdom.

What many people fail to see is that wherever you are and whatever role and responsibility you are playing inside your organization, you are only being judged on your ability to manage *that* role and the responsibilities that come with it. So be the best you can be and aim for the highest efficiency ratings, while managing your team well. Being one of the best at your current role will result in an opportunity to lead in a bigger role. Success does not come to anyone overnight; it requires great focus, learning, discipline, and years of experience to get there.

Having lofty goals is formidable. Knowing what it will take each day on the journey is important.

Key Takeaways

- The best leaders like David Morehouse train to face challenges, meet ambitious standards, hyper-learn, are adaptable, and persevere through trial and failure.
- Be accountable to yourself to maintain the standards.
- Exceed the standards by maximizing effort and contribution to your team.
- Learn valuable lessons from losses; you win or you learn.
- Confidence is a result of preparation and repetition.
- Master your current role and do your absolute best every day.

The Pain Exchange

Identify your superpowers and what separates you from others for branding, positioning, and maximizing your impact for a team. Answer these questions and plan for how you will maximize your contribution to your team.

1. List your top five skills you are most confident in. What have you done that you have extensive experience both in training and repetition?

2. What are you known for being the best at that you love doing and that gives you the most positive energy to stoke your inner desire? What are your three superpowers that you bring to a team or organization that will maximize your impact?

3. What accomplishment are you most proud of? And what did you have to overcome to attain the accomplishment? Remember, our stories shape our internal and external narratives. Synchronize stories of your accomplishments and what you had to overcome to attain them and to be known as a person of authenticity.

Place the answers on your one-page goal sheet of what you are looking to accomplish. These questions are your North Star to getting where you want to go. Align your personal and work goals accordingly.

Download the Bloom Growth™ One-Pager here: www.leadershipity.com/ThePlan.

3

The Formula for Great Teams Is People (and We All Need Them)

EVERYONE IN BUSINESS, organizations, and sports would like to have an effective team. And when I ask organizations "How is your team?" the inevitable answer is "Oh, we have a great team!" But the reality is that most teams are not actually all that good. So many organizations spend very little time acquiring or developing talent. One of the things I learned in pro sports was that a ton of effort, energy, and money is spent on finding the right players. And the best in the world at this—those whose only job is this primary responsibility—fail all the time. They miss, and many organizations miss. So thinking that your organization is thriving when you are not spending any time, focused effort, or money on it is bonkers!

I love what Bill Belichick has to say about teams:

"I'll know we have a great team when every person on the team knows their role and they are doing it."

This fabulous definition of high-quality teams is a remarkably simple one. I find that most organizations I work with often have both these challenges. First, I notice that several of the team members do not really understand their roles. No one who has been in a job for months should have to come to work every day and ask their direct supervisor, "What do you need me to do today?" This is a breakdown in training, specific communication guidelines, or unclear expectations for that person. Another issue is that, even when the roles are well defined, there may be no one holding the team members accountable, and they are thus not helping the team be the best they can be.

The Clarity Code

When an underperforming employee has no understanding or clarity on the reason they have been fired, this presents a challenging situation. I have seen this on several occasions. Clearly, there is a lack of communication regarding the role and/or a general misunderstanding of what they were responsible for.

Regular meetings or training at the start of a new role are defined, and often models of successful predecessors are held up for reference. Then monthly or quarterly reviews are held for accountability on the delivery and success in the current role. When you have an effective team with clear roles and responsibilities but team performance is suffering from their inability to deliver on these, you do not need to fire personnel because team members eliminate themselves. People tend to recognize when they are unable to do the job.

When organizations lay out all the demands, roles, and expectations and communicate what success looks like, they have what I call the *clarity code*. This is not an easy code to crack, but it is a crucial one to get done right!

Teams I work with are backed by a software called Bloom Growth™, which uses an interactive business operating system (BOS) to deliver focused execution and improved communications. It is a process where simplification and prioritization help the team get clarity, resulting in personal development within leaders and team members, which ultimately develops the strength of the entire team. It starts with a comprehensive approach to recognizing eight critical areas to an organization and rating each area on a scale of 1 to 10. I have yet to work with a team that takes a realistic assessment on day 1 and truly finds their organization at an 8, 9, or 10 in all these areas. Some of the eight areas may very well have an 8+ rating, but most fall below, which is why they recognize the organization and the team need help. Rating averages in the 5s are common. It's fine to be wherever you are on the journey, but these same groups in our initial call a week earlier tend to tell me, "We have a great team!" and one week later they've rated the organization a 5.5 out of 10!

These ratings are the simplest and most effective way to raise awareness of the gaps in teams that are limiting us from becoming the best we can be. Once you know where you are on this journey, you can develop a way to get where you really want to be, and understand what it will take to get there.

Five Behaviors of a Cohesive Team

I like Patrick Lencioni's *Five Behaviors of a Cohesive Team*. Out of his earlier book called *The Five Dysfunctions of a Team* came these five cohesive behaviors. I took training offered by Wiley, the publisher of this book, to be able to teach these five behaviors and the principles behind them to organizations. This is some of the best training that organizations can go through to help define their teams and build a high-quality foundation for their future. It also helps organizations and individuals decide who really wants to be on that team.

Trust: The biggest and most critical behavior of the five behaviors of a cohesive team triangle (Figure 3.1) is trust. It is the foundation of our organizations. I see organizations that are run very well, have quality leadership, have recruited very well, yet have an exceptionally low level of trust among their team. As a result, these teams are highly limited in what they can accomplish if trust is not established and built as a foundation. You do not have to be an expert builder to understand that a bad foundation is no place from which to start building.

TRUST ONE ANOTHER
When team members are genuinely transparent and honest with one another, they are able to build vulnerability-based trust.

ENGAGE IN CONFLICT AROUND IDEAS
When there is trust, team members are able to engage in unfiltered, constructive debate of ideas.

COMMIT TO DECISIONS
When team members are able to offer opinions and debate ideas, they will be more likely to commit to decisions.

HOLD ONE ANOTHER ACCOUNTABLE
When everyone is committed to a clear plan of action, they will be more willing to hold one another accountable.

FOCUS ON ACHIEVING COLLECTIVE RESULTS
The ultimate goal of building greater trust, healthy conflict, commitment, and accountability is one thing: the achievement of results.

Figure 3.1   Five behaviors of a cohesive team.

Conflict: The second layer of a cohesive team is conflict. It amazes me that most organizations do not have a plan, or rules of engagement, around conflict, because the last time I checked, most people have a job to do based on their expertise. So when conflict arises, we ask our personnel to resolve these challenges. Frankly, if there were no conflicts or challenges, I am not sure we would have as many employees, and you might not have a job! Solving conflicts may be our single largest contribution to a team.

Commitment: The third behavior factor is commitment. I repeatedly ask people, "Are you interested, or committed?" When we have great teams, everyone on that team is committed to their role, and that makes the team better because everyone is willing to take responsibility for what needs to be done. The difference is that people who are "interested" often talk, while those who are "committed" are doing and acting. Ownership and being present in our current roles are vital. It is also sometimes challenging for individuals to recognize that while they would like to be in a different role and feel they would be more successful in that role, they are only being judged on the current role they are responsible for.

Accountability: The fourth behavioral element is accountability. This is one of the largest "ity's" I have encountered. Accountability used to be standard in our practice of education, arts, in our homes, with our parents, and anyone who yielded any bit of authority, but nowadays it feels almost like a four-letter word! The people in positions of authority have left this key element out of their guidance and leadership, and the results have proven catastrophic. When we are talking about accountability for team members, I am focused on the accountability that members have to one another. This is the fourth tier of the cohesive team because if you get trust and productive conflict with a committed team, it is only natural for the team to want to hold one another accountable to the standards of the organization.

Results: The fifth and final element of cohesive team is results. Productivity (another big "ity") is a key measurement prevalent in our society. Yet it cannot be the first KPI we measure, because sustainable results only come after the first four elements of a cohesive team are done very well. Can you get satisfactory results without trust, commitment, conflict, and accountability? Yes, you can. The challenge is that the results are unlikely to be sustainable and repeatable.

As we look at the full scope of the behaviors of a cohesive team, there is a structure of value and importance in each of the five levels. Obviously, the surface area of the first three is much larger than the last two. Each level gets harder as you go but the first becomes a stepping stone for the second to build on, and each after the other, to ensure success at the next level and beyond.

Self-Belief

Jeff Blackman, Best-Selling Author, Broadcaster, and Member of the National Speaker Academy (NSA) Hall of Fame

For more than 18 years I have been directly and indirectly involved with the NSA, a fabulous organization that offers like-minded speakers a peer group with whom to spend effort in continuous improvement.

Jeff is an expert at delivering fabulous keynotes and offering training worldwide, and has authored a few wonderful books too.

Oddly, Jeff and I had never met prior to the recording, but we share a love of public speaking, education, travel, family, baseball, and business. Our one-hour timeslot on *Winners Find a Way* went by so quickly it felt like a 12-minute podcast!

TRENT: FOR A LEADER, WHAT IS THE ONE ATTRIBUTE THAT PREVAILS ABOVE THE REST?

Jeff: Everything in your life should be done to drive prominent levels of trust. That automatically reduces or eliminates fear from others when it comes to work in dealing with you.

IN ONE OF YOUR BOOKS YOU DISCUSS ORGANIZATIONS THAT EMBRACE *THE WIZARD OF OZ* PHILOSOPHY. CAN YOU EXPAND ON THAT?

Do I choose to imitate? Or do I choose to vegetate? And if you choose the latter, you don't want to do it. One of my Chicago clients suggested that is to abdicate. I always tell people, "If you always do what you've always done, you'll always get what you've always got for less." And I urge them not to embrace what I call *The Wizard of Oz* philosophy, which means no heart, no brain, no courage. Change requires courage, because you are entering the unknown.

WHAT HAS BEEN THE KEY TO INTEGRITY AND GETTING THE MINDSET RIGHT FOR A LEADER?

You don't cheat, you don't steal, you don't fudge; you do the right thing. And Bruce Jenner was so interesting, because when I asked him to tell me about the 1976 victory in Montreal for the decathlete gold medal, he said to me, "I didn't win the gold in 1976." And I looked at him kind of quizzically and said, "Bruce, it was 1976" (like I had to remind him when he won?). He clarified: "Jeff, in 1972 in Munich, I didn't win the gold. So I won the gold in 1972 when I lost by placing in my mind the fact that I, William Bruce Jenner, would be the next Olympic decathlete gold medal winner!" And here's what Bruce did. He took the pictures of the gold, silver, and bronze medalists, and he put a cutout of his face on the face of the gold medal winner from 1972, so he could visualize himself on the victory stand in 1976. And he said to himself, "I won in 1972, when I actually lost, because I wanted my mind to know that I believed in me, Jeff. So in Montreal, I didn't win the gold, I simply picked up a medal I had previously won." The power of goal achievement and visualization.

WHAT DO PEOPLE HAVE TO RECOGNIZE ABOUT BEING A LEADER FOR THEMSELVES?

I always stress to folks that your reputation reigns supreme.

IF PEOPLE ARE STRUGGLING OUT THERE TODAY, WHAT WOULD YOU TELL THEM THAT IS FOUNDATIONAL?

"I always stress to people in all aspects of your life—and this applies to you as a person and what's important to you, and it applies to relationships, with prospects, customers and clients, spouse, partner, significant other—when trust is high, fear is low."

– Jeff Blackman

High-Level Trust Equals Low-Level Fear

Organizations want to provide psychological safety at work. I had not heard the term "psychological safety" until several years ago because it's not a regular feature of competing sports teams. Intensity is high and the fear of being fired or cut often weighs on many people's minds. But fear is higher when trust is low. Thus we keep coming back to the ultimate value of trust. While this concept seems good and right, there is a deep challenge to my generation. Fear was a good teacher when I was in my teens and 20s. The consequences could be severe for not meeting your responsibilities and so there was a healthy fear of letting the team down, but also of facing repercussions and consequences. Sometimes repercussions and consequences were inconsistent, which meant lowered trust levels. Consistent leadership allows for the flow of energy. Trust should be the foundation you build on.

Know Your Team

As a leader, it is ultimately critical that you learn who your team members are. The best leaders in the world learn as much as possible about the team members they are going to bring into the organization, and how they will help them develop to serve the team for years to come. In an organization that requires much, knowing the abilities, strengths, and weaknesses of the team members is just the beginning of being able to lead your team well. As a leader, I am consistently calculating which of my team members is the right person for the challenges at hand and who has the skill set and mindset to achieve the tasks that lead to our goal. Leaders who do not really get to know their team members' capabilities, history, experiences, and skill sets commonly choose the wrong person for the task at hand. A leader willing to put in the time, effort, and understanding to communicate with their team members to learn about them is a defining factor in the team's success.

Overcoming Failure and Finding Balance
Chris Krause, NCSA Recruiting Founder; College Football
Player, Vanderbilt

Chris and I met in 2011 when I joined the Chicago chapter of
the Entrepreneurs' Organization (EO). A substantial number
of former athletes own companies, and my EO forum had five
Division I athletes among our nine members.

Chris and I served on the board of directors for EO
Chicago for a short stint, but our history in sports and his
recruiting firm marked us as kindred spirits. When I came out
of college, I wrote a business plan to build a recruiting firm for
high school athletes to find a way to land at a college that was
a good match for both the school and the athlete. I met Chris
15 years after vetting that plan with other entrepreneurs and
mentors I knew back in the mid-1990s. He had built it even
better than I had envisioned it!

Chris is a Chicago kid and grew up in a tough area; he was
a hard-nosed football player and overcame a lot of odds to
head off to Vanderbilt. While Vandy is not known for their
football program, it is one of the most academically acclaimed
universities in the United States.

Being so impressed with what Chris built and knowing his
history, I could not wait to have him on *Winners Find a Way*.

TRENT: WHAT WAS THE BIGGEST LEARNING THAT SEPARATED
YOU AT NCSA FROM A LOT OF COMPETITION IN THE
MARKETPLACE WHEN YOU STARTED?

Chris: One of our biggest challenges along the way was the
whole idea of failing fast. From the time that we had a system
in place at NCSA, we were having our scouts calling student
athletes directly. And then we switched the system where we

(continued)

(*continued*)

had a whole group—we had another division of people that call, that set meetings. We went from having appointment setters for the athletes, and then having the scouts actually meet the families, to saying just have the scouts call the families and we went to that. It did not work. Within two or three weeks, our production went down by about 50%, and we were at a point where the money was tight. And I had to write a check for $100,000 to cover payroll, because we didn't have enough money coming in.

We were on the verge of collapsing, and to be able to switch back and correct that immediately before it was too late. I mean, that is a failure recovery, which could have put the business under.

HAVING THAT TEAM ENVIRONMENT REALLY HELPED YOU RESPOND TO FAILURES FAST. CAN YOU GIVE AN EXAMPLE OF THE TEAM SACRIFICES?

We also had a thing, early in the company, when we had a database that we were putting together where we had a memory leak that caused us to lose our data. And for us to scramble and literally we worked 24 hours a day recouping and gathering back all these email addresses to all these college coaches to keep the integrity of that database.

The bottom line of that is when identifying what "it" is and putting a strategy together, and then putting in the time and the work to correct it—whether it be putting in the time and work in improving my bench-press or my 40 time back from high school—I always identified what were the weaknesses, and put a plan together to be in the category of what I needed to be successful. Those things come up all the time. And it is just a matter of looking at it as an opportunity to get better.

It is the same thing when you're lifting weights: if you lift weights all day long, and you do not go to failure where your muscles break down, you are never going to get stronger. It is the exact same thing as the human body.

SO HIRING MANY FORMER COMPETITIVE ATHLETES WHO UNDER-STOOD ROLES AND OVERCOMING FAILURE WAS KEY?

The whole idea of strength is that overuse can become a weakness. Knowledge can become a strength. I try to incorporate that in how I lead and find the people who are better than me at areas I'm not good at and bring them on the team.

DO YOU HAVE A GO-TO SAYING TO HELP KEEP THIS BALANCE FOR YOUR TEAM ALONG THIS JOURNEY OF LEADERSHIP?

The five characteristics of the championship team (from Sue Enqvist, UCLA softball coach and John Wooden mentee):

1. Vision: The coach paints the vision of where they're going. They're going to be champions; they know how they're going to get there.

2. Work ethic: How they are going to work, how they are going to work together, what offense and defense; they have a strategy.

3. Knowing the role or job: Everyone knows their position, what their job is, and how to do their job on their team. Do not try to do more than your job. If you're an offensive guard, don't try to be a wide receiver. If you're a center, you're getting rebounds and blocking shots. Don't be jacking up threes.

4. Safe space: Make it a safe place to fail, so if you do fail, everyone has your back.

5. Fun: The last thing is having fun.

And if you do those five things, you are going to have something special. And if you hold each other accountable,

(continued)

(*continued*)

when you see everybody together, when they win the championship, and they get together, they love each other. If there is a bond, there's love there and you want to work harder for your teammate than you want to work for yourself. That is when greatness is achieved.

> *"Embrace those failures. Have a team around you that wants to help because if you have the right team around you, when something goes wrong, other people on the team will step in, and help when a department is down or when a teammate falls. We help them get back up. And that is part of our culture; a culture that says, 'It's okay to fail, because that is how you grow.'"*
> — Chris Krause

Mindset Styles

One of the easiest measurements of a team member is whether they have a growth mindset or a fixed mindset. Both mindsets may have value for you, the team, and in your organization, given certain situations. But ultimately you must know which team members carry which mindset. For entrepreneurs, there are frequent cases where we are looking for team members with a growth mindset who can share in the vision and come alongside a growing team to create value. But when the process is essential and analytical detail that requires precision, such as in an accounting, architecture, or engineering project, I may need personnel with a fixed mindset to execute the process and procedure properly to deliver high-quality results repeatedly.

The Grit Formula

One of the other calculations I love in a team is the grit formula, which was made famous by author Angela Duckworth.

GRIT FORMULA (Effort counts twice!):

TALENT	×	EFFORT	=	SKILL
_____	×	_____	=	_____
(1–10)		(1–10)		(1–100)

SKILL	×	EFFORT	=	**ACHIEVEMENT**
_____	×	_____	=	_____
(1–100)		(1–10)		(1–1000)

LEADERSHIPITY Scale:
901 – 1000 = GOAT/Elite
701 – 900 = Top Leaders /Pro Performers
501 – 700 = C-suite/Leaders
401 – 500 = RDs/VPs
301 – 400 = Directors
201 + = Potential
<200 = DO NOT HIRE

To give you an example of this, I have coached several athletes who score 10 out of 10 on talent but 4 out of 10 for effort. That formula shows 10 (talent) × 4 (effort) = 40 (skill), 40 (skill) × 4 (effort) equals 160 (achievement). Imagine the scout after drafting someone in the first round who is so talented and finding out that most organizations would never hire and keep this person for over 60 days if they did. That would be what I would consider a flop, or failure, in a draft of a highly gifted and talented player.

When I think about a superstar like quarterback Tom Brady (often referred to as the GOAT—greatest of all time), his grit formula is a poster-chart for how to become one of the best in the world. Tom Brady was drafted out of college in the sixth round. He was clearly a good college football player at the University of Michigan, but his talent level on the NFL level was not initially viewed as remarkably high compared to other players at that time. I assume that Tom was probably considered a 6 out of 10 talent on the grit formula when he entered the league. It is likely an incredibly low talent rating for anyone drafted into the NFL. But where Tom Brady makes up for his *perceived* (that is all it is) lack of talent is in his effort, where he is a 10 out of 10, proving him to be a 600 straight out of the draft (6 × 10 = 60, 60 × 10 equals 600). Anytime this happens, that is an absolute steal of a draft choice that late in the sixth round.

As Tom Brady continued his journey in the NFL, a miraculous (but not surprising) thing happened along the way. His 6 rating out of 10 on talent soon became a 7 because his effort was at a level 10 on *every* rep, and this proved to be exactly what he needed to increase his talent. He was surrounded by the best coaches in the world who would help him develop that talent. A couple of years later, utilizing all that effort and great coaching gets him rated an 8 out of 10 in talent, and then later a 9. On that formula, 9 × 10 = 90; 90 × 10 = 900! Nine hundred is often viewed as the absolute best in their organization and often in their area of expertise.

> "We judge ourselves on our intentions, and we judge others on their actions."
>
> – Stephen M.R. Covey

An exercise I love to do with the grit formula is to have an organization's team members come in and rate themselves on their own talent and effort level and compare that to what their direct supervisors and executive team rate them, and how I rate them as well. There is often a gap in self-realization between how they see themselves and how others see them.

This is an excellent way to have a very frank, open dialogue and develop clarity with our team members to help them know exactly where they are right now given their current role and for what they are responsible. And then discuss how they can raise that level and what that looks like, which can be defined by behaviors, KPIs, models of past success, and any measurement that you see fit that can be graded and measured accordingly.

Tough Times Don't Last; Tough People Do

Steve Lombardo III, College Baseball, Georgetown; CEO, Gibsons Restaurant Group

When I joined EO Chicago in 2011, I was tapped to join the board to become the mentorship chairperson. Each month our board meetings were held at world-famous Gibsons Bar & Steakhouse on Rush Street. Steve Lombardo was both a member of EO and the owner of a major wine importer with a company called Blue Star, and his family-owned Gibsons Restaurant Group. GRG is consistently in the top three privately held restaurant groups in the country. He was also a partner at Katten Muchin Rosenman LLP, one of the most prestigious law firms in Chicago.

We are kindred spirits in both our passion for the game of business and as college baseball players. Steve played first base and the outfield for Georgetown. I welcomed Steve on *Winners Find a Way*, and with his extensive background, I could have interviewed him for hours.

TRENT: YOU HAVE SEEN MANY TRIALS IN YOUR MANY YEARS IN BUSINESS AS AN IMPORTER, WORKING WITH CLIENTS AS AN M&A ATTORNEY, AND NOW THE FAMILY BUSINESS YOU ARE CEO OF, THE GIBSON GROUP, FACED A PANDEMIC THAT COULD FEASIBLY DESTROY EVERYTHING YOUR FAMILY WORKED SO HARD FOR. HOW DO YOU RESPOND?

Steve: When it comes to a difficult time, like the pandemic for restaurants, I will say that in times of stress and adversity people's true characters come out for good, and for bad. We found out pretty quickly who was on the team and who wasn't. Most of the people were on the team and there were some people that very clearly indicated they were not. That's one of those times in life and you don't get an opportunity like that very often.

(continued)

(*continued*)

SEEING YOUR PEOPLE RALLY AND STAYING TRUE TO THE VALUES
OF GIBSONS, WELL KNOWN FOR THEIR CULTURE, WALK US
THROUGH THE POSITIVE OUTCOME FROM YOUR TEAM'S RESPONSE.

I do think we worked out deals with vendors, we worked out deals with landlords. But we also tried to be fair; we weren't trying to take advantage of the situation in any way, shape, or form. We wanted to be fair to our landlords.

And it is one of the great opportunities in a crisis and on any major challenge, it can really bond people together. Like when we are talking about the military and the bond of brothers and people going through adversity together and how it bonds people. It was something like that with our teams. It can go one of two ways. It can tear people apart if you don't manage it well. But you see people taking care of each other and those bonds become close. And then you're not just doing it for the business or for the paycheck; you're doing it for the person who's next to you, who's on this side of you, because she needs help. And you are helping her because that bond is there as a team.

BRINGING THE ICONIC BRAND THROUGH AN EPIC AND
HOPEFULLY ONCE-IN-A-LIFETIME CHALLENGE, WHAT DO YOU FEEL
LIKE THE LEADERS DID WELL THAT SEPARATED YOUR TEAM
FROM OTHERS?

I do think communication is a key piece of it. Because with 2,200 people, you have 2,200 ideas. Listen to your people because they will have ideas that will help. Plenty of ideas that will not work. But that is one of 2,200. It was not just a feeling. There was a little bit of stress at the very beginning, like, "How is this happening? Why is this happening?" I wouldn't even call it feeling sorry for ourselves; it is just sort of like being hit with shock. But then it's just rolling up your sleeves and

> getting down to it. There is no choice, and that is what you have to do. Just get into it!
>
> *"In times of stress and adversity people's true characters come out for good, and for bad."*
> — *Steve Lombardo III*

Assess the Members

There are many tools out there to determine which team members are the best fit for your organization. I have used Wiley's DiSC Assessments: Work of Leaders for the executive team members and top of the organization chart. Wiley also has a candidate search tool called PXT Select to assist in making better personnel choices. Many of my clients incorporate the Culture Index. Angela Duckworth's grit formula is also useful. There are many options in how you might choose to train up and assess your talent and help your team members, and ultimately the team, get better.

Making an industry-specific choice may be beneficial, but choose a tool that can be something that creates value for your team members and team to use for a consistent reference and that will help you take your team to the next level of becoming great! Culture Index, Enneagram, and Myers-Briggs have tons of data and I see these regularly in use by organizations.

Key Takeaways

- Data often contradicts assertions that you have a great team in place.
- Train your team with clearly defined roles and responsibilities for each team member and implement regular team member reviews for accountability.
- Build teams using the five behaviors of a cohesive team.
- Leaders should know their team members well.

- Individuals trained in teamwork, like athletes, make valuable team members.
- Good teams cultivate a culture of support, rallying around each other.
- Choose effective assessment tools.

The Pain Exchange

Decide which assessment(s) you are going to use to determine and monitor helping your team become the best they can be. You could also have one you are already using or one that you create specific to your values and descriptions of what a great teammate looks like in your organization.

1. Take *all* the assessments as leaders first and have solid self-awareness. Take note of the three items that each of the leaders could improve on as a teammate and model leadership by building daily action to improve these items for you and your teammates

2. Add these improvements to be a part of your quarterly goals to hold one another accountable for being better leaders and models for your organization and fellow team members.

3. Have personnel use these tools and take these assessments. I also highly recommend a peer-to-peer review or 360 assessment for key personnel who are interactive and have major influence on team members, vendors, clients, and leadership.

4. Review the results, plus suggested action steps, and incorporate those into the team member's goals and regular performance reviews.

Advanced Pain Exchange: Team Health Day

Book a Five Behaviors of a Cohesive Team Training for your organization at Trent@leadershipity.com.

4

Understanding and Leading Team Members

KNOWING YOUR TEAM members and having a profile on each person is a big deal to me. Being a good coach often comes down to knowing your team members very well. It's very important for an organization and its leaders to look at their team and have a ton of data and background on each member. We are constantly making decisions based on our personnel, and as a coach I am consistently putting my members in a position to be successful.

Baseball Cards for Your Team Members

The first thing I start with is a background on each individual person within the organization. They are the folks I will be managing first. I build a profile on my peers, my bosses, the ownership group—I want a significant profile for every single person I'm going to encounter. Where do they come from, where were they raised, what was family life like growing up, what university did they go to? Did they go to trade school? How do they learn? What motivates them? What are their superpowers? Where do they think they will have maximum impact and contribute the most?

These details will give you clarity of where people are coming from. It is a beautiful way to dive into the lens of how someone sees the world and from their experiences. I did not have the same

experiences as many of my teammates and team members and that
is okay. They did not have the same experiences I had either. I love
the fact that we come from diverse backgrounds and those experiences shaped our lens and our view of the world and how we manage the things in front of us.

The Human Experience

Once I was passed over for not being an "appropriate" person for a DEI
(diversity, equity, and inclusion) panel. I was frustrated by that. I am a
guy who won a world championship with 50 different people on a team,
from five countries, speaking four different languages, and from all sorts
of economic and diverse backgrounds. All worked together as a team
with one goal. And each team member worked to figure out their role
and their best way to create impact for the team and the organization
to be successful regardless of age, sex, economic, or educational background. While these things may be factors in people's lives, none of
them preclude someone from participating, and actually the diversity
adds value to the team and to the experience. I like to call this the
human experience. I want to know how someone got here, what road
was taken to this point. Tell me about your journey.

Talent Can Only Take You So Far

Mark Gallagher, Founder and Co-owner of Status Grand
Prix; Head of Marketing, Formula 1 Team; Founding
Member, Red Bull Formula 1 Racing

*"Talent can only take you so far. The most successful people
make it a priority to build relationships and rapport with their
team because they know that without their crew and support
staff, they could never reach such great heights."*
                                              – Mark Gallagher

Mark and I met at a social event during an EO trip to
Shanghai, where I was presenting at NYU on mentorship and

Mark gave an inspirational talk on how teams work together efficiently.

Mark is a Formula 1 (F1) expert who lives in London and has many good insights into teams and relationships based on his vast knowledge of the pits and as a founding member of the Red Bull F1 Racing Team.

The sport has evolved dramatically over the years and remains one of the most popular sports on the globe. Mark discussed the area in the UK where many teams, such as Mercedes, Williams, Red Bull, McLaren, Haas, Alpine, and Aston Martin, all have their main engineering facilities and headquarters.

I asked Mark to come on *Winners Find a Way* to discuss his experience, detailed in his book, *The Business of Winning*.

TRENT: YOU ARE IN ONE OF THE MOST PROLIFIC SPORTS IN THE WORLD, WHICH BRINGS BOTH GLAMOUR AND SOMETIMES UNHEALTHY CRITICISM. WHAT HAVE YOU LEARNED ABOUT YOUR TEAM THROUGH THIS ULTIMATE PERFORMANCE AND MEASURED SPORT?

Mark: One of the things about working in a top-line professional sport like Formula 1, from a leadership point of view, is when you work in the senior management role it can become quite easy to criticize some of the folks you employ to design these cars, to engineer these cars, and indeed to drive the cars. And we talk about the difference in performance of a few tenths of a second. You find yourself inevitably joining everyone in criticizing the driver who's maybe four-tenths of a second per lap slower than his Formula 1 teammates, or some other incredibly small margin of performance.

When you actually drive these cars, you come to realize that all these people who drive them are on a different level, and they are all doing an amazing job. So therefore, it's quite a

(continued)

(continued)

good experience to humble yourself by driving one of them and then realizing that even the driver who appears to be a little bit off the pace at the top of Formula 1 is actually doing an amazing job. And they're all highly skilled at what they do.

WHERE DO YOU SEE CHALLENGES FROM UNDERPERFORMING TEAM MEMBERS?

If you stop one of those drivers who is not extracting their full potential and you were to tell them that, they will argue with you. They would say, "Yeah, but I do everything. I train, I'm physically fit enough. I attend all the meetings; I do everything I've been asked to do." Of course, there is the problem. It should not be what you're asked to do; you should be going the extra mile yourself.

WHAT IS THE DANGER OF "BELIEVING YOUR OWN PRESS CLIPPINGS" AFTER SUCCESS IN SUCH A POPULAR SPORT?

If at a young age you're surrounded by people who tell you that you are kind of brilliant to the point where you begin to believe your own PR, you begin to believe there is nothing that you need to learn. That's a very dangerous place to go into because we all keep learning. I'm still learning now, and you should never get to the point where you believe that you know everything.

WHAT HAVE YOU LEARNED ABOUT TEAM COMMITMENT AND TEAM RELATIONSHIPS?

The difficulty in F1 is that it is such a wealthy global sport that some of the race car drivers when they get to F1 really do believe that they have arrived. They are at the pinnacle or the top of the heap. And that brings the danger when they start to look down on everyone, and that is just asking for trouble. I mean you might be earning a hundred times more than the mechanic who builds your car but if the mechanic who builds your car doesn't come to work with the same level of commitment as you bring, you've got a problem.

So let's forget the material wealth differences. Let's focus on the fact that we're all team members together. I think for the drivers who just miss it, they get into that privileged position early in their career and they stop learning, and that is a sure way to make sure that you are never going to achieve your potential.

Not an Interrogation

Learning about a person's background should not feel like an interrogation or legal deposition where you're going to run somebody through a hard line of questioning. This can be very simply a talk over lunch while traveling together. Ask the questions and learn something about their family, their educational path, if they've taken personality tests before. What is their personality style from the results, both personally and professionally? What kind of learner are they? Tactile? Can they read something and get it right away? Are they an audible learner and can hear something and know that information immediately? Do they have a photographic memory and can read this once and always remember the information? All those questions about someone help me set up my training and expertise on how I'm going to bring my team members along to get them better, and where to place them in our work to assure they are successful.

Mission Words

Dave Wannstedt, Head NFL and Collegiate Coach, Chicago Bears, Miami Dolphins, and University of Pittsburgh; Football Analyst, Fox

When I lived in Chicago, I regularly attended a weekly Bible study with a CRU ministry leader and fellow professionals who

(continued)

(*continued*)

either worked or lived in the city. Both Dave and I were regular attendees when we were in town. Dave coached young men for years but was also one of those young men as a player at the University of Pittsburgh back in his prime. Pretty cool to have played in college and the NFL and then coached at both levels too.

I asked Dave to share some wisdom he had gleaned over the years. At that time, he was sharing his insights as an analyst every weekend on Fox Sports.

TRENT: WHAT HAVE YOU FELT WAS THE STRONGEST ATTRIBUTE YOU WANT TO SEE IN YOUR PLAYERS?

Dave: There are only so many things that you can control. You cannot control how tall you are, maybe how smart you are, how fast you are, but you can control your work ethic and how much effort you can put into things.

WHAT WAS ONE OF THE BIGGEST CHALLENGES IN GETTING YOUR PLAYERS IN ALIGNMENT?

How am I going to get these 11 guys on offense or defense to do what we have to do to win? And they know what we have to do. But none of them really wanted to do it, whether it be the running or the lifting or the practices or whatever it was. You learn that everybody has different buttons that you push and your motivation for one guy might be completely different for another guy.

WHAT WAS ONE THING THAT YOU FELT HAD THE MOST IMPACT ON GETTING 75 PLAYERS TO GET ALIGNED, EVEN THOUGH YOU RECOGNIZED DIFFERENT MOTIVATIONS FOR EACH OF YOUR PLAYERS?

"I always had two or three words. And I would put those words in the meeting rooms, in the bathrooms, in the training

rooms, in the weight rooms. And those two or three words I would probably tie in 75% of the time in my talks to the team. I called them mission words."

— *Dave Wannstedt*

The words weren't drastically different, but they were a little different for college maybe than they were for the NFL, but you come up with something that really relates to the situation you are in. Because one job you are taking is where it is a winning program and they are going into the playoffs, then another job you take is where they haven't won in a long time. So your mission words, as I call them, would be a little different. And so that was always a big part of what I did.

WHAT HAS BEEN A KEY ELEMENT YOU REQUIRE OF YOUR PLAYERS TO BUILD YOUR TEAM CULTURE AND UNITY?

Are you doing everything you can to try to correct the situation yourself? Are you getting in there with a positive attitude? I have always talked about positive attitude, plus effort. If you're giving great effort and you've got a terrible attitude, you're not going to maximize the situation. Be positive about it and give a great effort.

WHAT HAS BEEN THE BIGGEST DOWNFALL FROM LEADERSHIP TO UPSET THE DIRECTION OF YOUR TEAM?

One big danger as a leader is overpromising. It's easy to get caught up when you add a new player or add a new coach. I used to say, "Let's not go out there and try to win the press conference and get everybody excited." Sometimes things don't work out and people don't understand that, and they don't care. So, on the overpromising thing, several times I've gotten trapped because I've gotten so excited about something we were doing.

Motivation and Prioritization

Dave Wannstedt recognized the values that he was looking for in his team members of a strong work ethic, positive attitude, and getting the players aligned on their motivations toward prioritizing on his two or three key concepts—his mission words. He works diligently to get values aligned to key priorities, and expects the players to find their way to get on board.

What are a team member's individual goals and what are they trying to accomplish? Knowing what drives somebody is so important. I like that if I know what my team members are going for, I can help them get there and come alongside and be an asset to them, knowing exactly what they would like to achieve. It also shapes our direct conversations. I will find out what is important to them. For example, if they're leading with the almighty dollar as very important, and say something like, "I grew up poor and now I just want to have enough money that I don't ever have to worry about not being able to make rent, missing meals, having warm clothes, or garments that fit," then I need to meet them right where they are knowing that monetary stability is a motivator. I use their language in breaking down why the drills are important and how reviewing the video will get them an extension to their contract and how a little more preparation will translate into better performance. This gives them the opportunity for a multiyear agreement, with a bigger paycheck.

It is so important for us to understand what our team members value. Find out what is acceptable for them and what is not. Sometimes it is as simple as asking, "What's not tolerated around you?" There will be all sorts of answers to that question, and that is not to say that they do not show some of those characteristics that we dislike or disagree with. I do not care for dishonesty, but I have been dishonest before. I do not care for lazy actors who fall out of shape as top-performing athletes, but I have gained weight in certain seasons of my life. We all falter, and we all make errors, but this is rare for A-team-level players. What they think is important is critical to aligning with the values of your organization, and how they are going to align with the values of their team members, as well as model those values. All become extremely important if I'm looking at an A-team member profile and bringing A-team members along. They walk the walk and talk the talk by their own standards.

Four Keys to a Strong Foundation

Trust is that foundation of building a good team. We talked a little bit about that foundation in the previous chapter, but I would like to talk about the four keys of trust building: *confidentiality, vulnerability, authenticity,* and *dependability.*

Confidentiality is critical. If you tell a person something, will they hold that in confidence? We must know that we can talk to our teammates about things that are especially important to us and know that it will not get back to everyone on our team, or to our boss, or to a client, or anyone else along the line. If they do not hold that in confidence, our trust is broken. And that is a challenge. It's hard to build a solid relationship on distrust. Without trust, there are cracks in the foundation. And once there are cracks, anything you try to build up will likely break the foundation and end up crashing.

Second in trust building is vulnerability. People who are willing to show a vulnerable side are more trustworthy. They show that they are giving you something particularly important and near and dear to them when they share that information. And it is a moment of vulnerability. Likely the very willingness to give vulnerability means they can usually manage people showing them vulnerability in return, and others appreciate that. On the other side, any person who uses that information against the other person is not someone you are going to trust in the future.

Being an authentic and genuine person is the third key in building trust. If you are a person who walks the walk and talks the talk, you are a person of your word. And when you say something, that means you are going to make every effort to ensure that you make that something a reality. If you tell me you are going to have something done by Friday at 2:00 p.m., and you are a person of your word, you are going to do it by 2:00 p.m. on Friday.

The final key to trust building is dependability. People who are dependable are often seen as trustworthy. We can rely on them to accomplish things that we need done.

I like to surround myself with winners, and winners can always be trusted and carry these four characteristics.

Network and Connection

Our lives are filled with relationships, some that come and go and others that are long-lasting. It takes a concerted effort to keep your network engaged and involved. To stay engaged with all the people you know can be a challenge. As your network grows, start a vlog, blog, a Facebook group, or LinkedIn page where you can pump content to your network in a bulk format. I use a weekly email newsletter to keep my large network in the loop. I am faithful in making sure the information exchanged can add value to them. Educate, inspire, or entertain your network. If your posts or information are all about you, it is unlikely they will stay tuned. Keep a public-facing calendar so that your network can see when you'll be in town, or back with familiar people. Post and welcome people to reach out and connect while in town. Even if you cannot meet in person, it is an interaction to your network and another chance to stay in touch with your network.

As a public speaker, I commonly run into people in a coffee shop who begin talking to me like they've known me for years. I'm often vexed that I don't recognize the person, who may only have seen me speak on a stage or to a group.

When I do speak, I speak from the heart with a genuine and authentic manner to build trust, so people often feel they know me well and are building a profile on who I am in their mind. I don't want to have an onstage persona and something different in my actual life. I am not an actor. And the information is not all fun and rosy, because I do share from a vulnerable standpoint and from many errors and challenges I have faced. I think it is important to be balanced, to explore both the good and the dreadful things, because we learn from both.

I meet these people in random places so I don't have a profile on them, but they have a profile on me, even if it's an informal one. When they tell me where and when they saw me, whom they work for within an organization, or how we know each other, that certainly helps further the conversation and build familiarity. But the fact remains that they have a lot more familiarity with me than I do with them.

It Is Not "Who You Know"

For a long time in professional baseball, I was told, "It's all about who you know!" First, I do not believe that at all. I believe it *is* who knows you! I know a lot of people who do not know me. And when I'm putting down a reference for a job opportunity, or someone is giving me a testimonial about the work or service I've offered for their organization, they're going to tell someone how they know me to be—my talent, attitude, character, and effort levels. They do know me, but "how they know me to be" becomes really evident and important at this point. So when my letters of reference go out and someone calls that person, it is not who I know. It is how they know me to be: "a person who can have impact inside an organization." When called, will they say, "He is a diligent person who is authentic, can hold confidentiality, and is vulnerable, dependable, and truthful," proving that I am trustworthy? Will they say, "He gives his best effort"? Will they say, "He's a lifelong learner"? Will they say, "He's committed to continuous improvement"?

When the New York Yankees had a job opening, I realized that I knew Mr. Steinbrenner, the owner, but he didn't know me. I needed a strong reference to endorse me, someone influential in the organization. If a good friend or Yankees' coach had introduced me to Mr. Steinbrenner previously on my trips into New York as a Tiger, Indian, or Angel, and we had built a friendly relationship, the opportunity might have looked different. Mr. Steinbrenner might then have told his GM, "I know this young strength coach from the LA Angels who has already been in three World Series by the age of 32, and he has a reputation as a diligent worker and keeps his players on the field. I think we should take a good look at him filling this opening." That would have been a game-changer. So it turns out that it is not who I *know*; it is who *knows* me and how they know me to be.

Judge Not Lest Ye Be Judged

As a young man, I was working hard to build my career. I wanted to get to the major leagues, my first goal. I was extremely judgmental of what people thought was demanding work, how they carried themselves, and if their values aligned with my values. It was an immature approach, and looking back I realize it was one of pride—and selfishness.

As I have grown in my spiritual faith, I have learned that there will be judgment someday for all of us, but I'm not qualified to render judgment on others. I heard an interview a few years back with Josh Hamilton—a number one pick overall and a young man with tons of talent who was deemed the next great power hitter in baseball at 17 years old—talking about his troubled times. He became addicted to drugs and alcohol during his minor league development after serious off-field trials in his life. In the interview, Josh talked about one day sitting in a tattoo parlor and looking around, when he realized, "I was with good people who were making bad decisions." That really resonated with me. Josh ended up having a good major league baseball career, but that fell far below the highly touted expectations as "one of the best players ever" when he was drafted.

I am not qualified to determine who are good people and who are bad people. I do not want to have to make those choices and decisions, and again, I do not think I'm qualified to make them. If someone asked me, "Are you a good person?" I would think that yes,

I am a good person. But I can also think of things I've done that may prove otherwise—errors I've made, people I mistreated, or times I stepped across a line that I knew was on the wrong side of integrity. So does that make me a bad person? I'm not sure. I try not to get bogged down in the question of good or bad, but rather to stay focused on the task at hand, and what I need to get it done.

"Be curious, Not judgmental."

– **Unknown**

I love this quote. It really has shaped me, even though I heard it for the first time when I was over 50 years old!

Visibility

Leaders set a higher standard for themselves and model that higher standard, one that should exceed the team members' standards. As we look at our team and we have built the profiles of our team members, it is so important to be visible to them and model the standards we stand for. Leaning into those relationships with communication and openness is essential, both to continue to develop your team and for them to have a good solid working relationship that is open and honest. Holding yourself accountable to your own standards is the first step before you hold other people accountable to those same standards.

Key Takeaways

- Encourage individuals to go the extra mile for the collective benefit.
- Avoid arrogant behavior and complacency in yourself and others.
- Maintain a balanced team without unnecessary hierarchy; emphasize that every team member, regardless of role, plays a crucial part.

- Build profiles on team members to understand their motivations, learning styles, values, and what drives them—recognize their human side.
- Establish a sturdy foundation of trust for the team through confidentiality, vulnerability, authenticity, and dependability.
- Stress the importance of networking and staying connected to remain relevant.
- Be visible to your team and set higher standards for yourself, demonstrating excellence and exceeding expectations.

The Pain Exchange

Build team profiles for each member on your team. Format it to a structure of less than two pages (or a one-pager that has information front and back):

- Use a CRM for a reference of some key elements you'd like to have in the profile.
- Include information on background, present status, and future outlook.
- Make this document easy for fellow team leaders to update and access.
- Identify any industry-specific data points, such as certifications, continuing education credits, licenses, credentials, and so on.

Know your team members. I love the quote "If you want the right answers, you must ask the right questions." Because I am asked to put team members in a position to be successful, I want the right information from each team member to know how I can position them to be successful.

Download a sample one-pager at www.leadershipity.com/profile.

5

The Journey to Excellence (with a Few Stops in Mediocrity)

LEADERS WITH LOW standards produce minimum achievers. I have rarely seen a performer meet the expectations of a boss or a superior and then absolutely blow past that standard to two times the expectations of the organization. Perhaps it's human nature, but most folks get right up to that standard, surpass it to a minimal level by 10 or 20%, and then rest on their laurels; they don't keep pushing that limit to expand to the next level. For example, I often see salespeople hit their quota for the quarter and if they do that after two months, they will take vacation and not do much for the third month because they've already made their quota. They may not be incentivized to continue pushing, and that's an issue with the organization's standards.

A Low Bar

What I have found is that when people surpass the standard easily, a "losing" behavior takes over if they are not challenged to "go the extra mile" or compensated for it. The losing behaviors of excuses, blame, quitting, and ignoring data become more prevalent. Leaders must recognize that top performers are motivated by stretching the boundaries and meeting the top challengers. If an organization is

73

unable to keep these top performers engaged, they tend to lose them to another organization, or their productivity drops off out of boredom.

For the folks who are indifferent to the standards, I see that they avoid comparison and do not want to compete or be held accountable to the standards. Such people want accolades for performance, but if they are not performing well, or at the standard people consider to be high-quality work, they are jealous, envious, and oppose any accolades given to others. I have seen this play out in an attitude of "grace for me and justice for everyone else."

It reminds me a bit of the quote I included in Chapter 3: "We judge ourselves on our intentions, and we judge others on their actions." How does this show up?

- You want to be judged that you tried for the standard and intended to meet it. So you had good intentions (though you never took the actions requested of you).
- You immediately grab hold of the four or five other people who didn't meet the standard and are very harsh about the fact they also didn't meet the standard and should probably be fired, or at least be reprimanded. Often, you're extremely fierce about others not making the standard but will ask for forgiveness for yourself not making it because you feel inside that your intent was to get there.

A High Standard Is the Only Standard

The lessons I learned in my journey were many, but from the time I was 16 years old until I was 27, there were seven different championship runs in those years. It was interesting to see both sides, from being mediocre to competing for titles. In that journey I learned that the coaches held a high standard and expectations for team members. They were developing competitive teams and higher-level standards of competition.

In contrast, teams that did not require high standards and offered low levels of accountability and little visibility, as well as poor communication, resulted in unclear expectations of goals and values. This was a recipe for mediocrity at best. At the worst, failure. The great organizations had coaches that would give a message of solidarity that the entire staff supported and communicated difficult and challenging times ahead. And their work was solely focused on making that goal or process come to fruition and into a reality for each athlete.

In high school, the expectation was to compete for a state title every year. My college tennis coach fully felt we could compete for the national championship and expected us not only to get there but to win it. Coach Nick Saban and Coach Tom Izzo expected the organization to be the best it could be, and the standards were set extremely high for an organization that had not competed often at the level that these men held as "the consistent standard" prior to their arrival.

King of the Mountain

My journey took me from organizations that were both trying and committing to getting better—like most organizations—to other organizations that had already arrived and were at the peak of their development standards. At times I was at the top and we were the team that everybody wanted to knock off. And at other times I was playing or coaching from the middle or the bottom, where we were just trying to get competitive and attempting to become a playoff-level team.

In Cleveland, with the *Indians* in the mid-1990's, everyone felt the goal was very public—within the organization, within the city limits, within the fan base, within the vendors that worked for the team, and within the competition—and this provided clarity. The owner, staff, and leadership group did not hesitate to let everybody know what they were going for and welcomed all comers to knock them off that goal. Bring the world title to Cleveland! It certainly looked like a level of arrogance at the time. Looking back, I would equate it to a significant level of confidence in the ability of the team members, the staff, the resources available, and the attitudes and belief in the players. The standards set were extremely high and anything less than a world title was unacceptable.

The Power of One
Dave Andrews, Chairperson, Board of Governors, and President, AHL (retired)

Dave served as the president of the American Hockey League (AHL) for over 25 years. He entered the AHL Hall of Fame in 2021 and has been bestowed with too many awards to list here for his service to pro hockey.

It's fun to sit down with someone of Dave's longevity to hear his stories of how the game has progressed throughout different generations. When we invited Dave for an interview, he was extremely accommodating and gracious with his time. The full interview is filled with gems of wisdom.

TRENT: YOU STARTED OUT IN THE COACHING RANKS, LEARNING VALUABLE LESSONS OF CULTURE VERSUS PRODUCTIVITY. CAN YOU SHARE AN EXAMPLE?

Dave: I was kind of putting production over the team harmony, and that was a mistake.

"Recognizing the influence of a single person—how one team member can lead, empower, and set the tone for the rest of the team (positively or negatively). I learned not to put production over team harmony."

– Dave Andrews

WHAT WAS ONE OF MOST VALUABLE LESSONS FOR LEADERS THAT YOU LEARNED?

Part of managing the expectations of a team is holding yourself to elevated expectations. Coaches and managers cannot expect the team to work hard if they don't. I had a couple of coaches who were not prepared, who did not put in the kind of effort they were demanding or the standards they had for their players that they weren't living up to themselves. And I think when a coach doesn't put in the sort of effort that they need to, it really shows how they judge talent and use their personnel. You lose trust in the decision-making of that person.

WHAT IS ONE OF THE KEY ELEMENTS OF SHOWING YOUR TEAM THAT YOU CARE AND ARE TAKING ACTION?

We are always at some point in a strategic planning cycle. When we go through a performance appraisal cycle with our staff, when it is fully complete, I'll come back and identify things raised through performance reviews by employees here and tell them what we plan to do about it. And then the next time we get together, it's not what we plan to do about it but that we did it. So I think it's a continuous planning process where you can show results. It tells your stakeholders you care. It tells them you are not sort of stuck in a set of work plans that don't change.

ALIGNMENT TO A VISION IS TOUGH THESE DAYS TO BUILD IN ANY ORGANIZATION. HOW ARE YOU FACING THAT INSIDE YOUR TEAM?

When you fall out of alignment, which happens with a strategic vision, you must look back and see who is falling out of alignment and why. And get back and deal with that particular

(continued)

(*continued*)

group of people or that particular individual one-on-one and say, "Look, this is where we're trying to go; this is why we're trying to get there." I mean, you should, as a leader, be able to support that in conversation, say what the reason is that you are unable to support this, and ask what I can do to get your support.

Because it is important for us to get to this end vision. But you must do a kind of trackback just like a coach does to the fundamentals. One thing I have learned as a coach is if you assume that the fundamentals are there year after year because you taught the team some sort of fundamental of your system or break out one year ago and you think that is still going to be there a year later, forget it. You must keep revisiting the vision. You have to keep revisiting those issues that are challenging the vision, find out why, and work as hard as possible to change the thinking and bring them into alignment. And if you're unsuccessful with that, you may be able to use other people within your group to influence them, or you may just decide you've got to move on, and you're not going to have full-force sort of consensus, but you're going to have enough to move forward.

Comprehensive Conditioning

I believe that from this journey of excellence, four levels of conditioning are required. And it is a holistic, or comprehensive, way of thinking about how I am going to train my team. When I think about training and improvement, we categorically look at areas of expertise and areas that are critical to the success of our role. Say that you have six areas to train your team for. If one or two of those areas are strong and you are spending a lot of time and energy to improve those two strongest areas but are perhaps neglecting the other four, it tends to have a mediocre or less than average result.

We can be great at these two things, but if we are poor at these other four things then that does not create a lot of balance. As we develop, we want to keep moving the needle up in all six areas, getting better every time in *all* these areas.

Four Critical Areas

There are four areas of conditioning that I believe are critical for training to be excellent: *moral, mental, physical,* and *emotional.* We must develop our integrity and moral character first; it is foundational. And then we develop our mental thinking capacity and mindset second. Then we move to the physical conditioning as a stepping stone to be prepared for what is about to happen and our health and wellness. But our emotional conditioning is critical to understanding and growing our maturity and how we are navigating our emotions through work, play, communication, leadership, and so on. (Note that you can work on emotional conditioning before physical conditioning and still come out on top. Invert three or four anytime and feel good about it.) You can apply different standards and KPIs for each critical area.

- Moral conditioning:
  - Begin a weekly book or Bible study with like-minded leaders whom you admire and who share your values and beliefs.
  - Attend a weekly service with a congregation and community that share your beliefs.
  - Read 10 pages per day of inspirational and uplifting material on character and spiritual development.
  - Pray with your children and spouse before bed.

- Mental conditioning (do each for 90 days):
  - Journal daily in gratitude on at least three things, with two of those being about people in life for whom you are thankful.

o Plan one area of focus to improve on during practice/ work/dinner for each workday.
o Improve focus by eliminating phone scrolling to no more than 10 minutes per day and set timers on social media usage.

- Physical conditioning (do each for 90 days):
  o Perform morning workouts of 30 minutes each or more, four days per week.
  o Drink 100 oz of water per day.
  o Walk over two miles three times per week.
  o Plan workouts and get a training buddy for both workouts.

- Emotional conditioning:
  o Journal for 10 minutes at the end of each day on how you managed your emotions in situations for the day; how you were feeling at the time; how you responded and your response to certain situations; and how your self-talk was during the event.
  o Do 10 minutes of meditation each morning before beginning the day with no less than 20 deep breaths (in through the nose and out through the mouth, 10 seconds minimum per breath).
  o Attempt one new craft, skill, or hobby you have never done, such as needlepoint, juggling, pickleball, scrapbooking, hunting, distance swimming, or something else.

The Big "Ity"

As we talk about our integrity, we focus on self-awareness and the standards set for the organization, but our personal standards should always be set well above the organizations to maintain the integrity we are looking for. And having awareness around areas in your life that are struggles and how you are going to challenge and tackle those things in your life is crucial.

I do not believe that everyone does everything well. In fact, most people have areas that trip them up. Having self-awareness around the fact that your style may rub people the wrong way in some aspect is important, as I have learned from leaders who recognize these challenges through self-awareness. It's important to make people aware that you have a challenge and admit, "I don't do this very well. And if you feel I'm not doing it very well, for you or for the team, I give you permission to let me know when my behavior is poor, or when I'm not meeting expectations, or not meeting the standard because I have been guilty of it before."

One of the biggest challenges in people's relationships is a lack of self-awareness for behaviors that show up and offend people. If you have been guilty of this yet feel it is misinterpreted, giving people permission to address it with you when you are showing these behaviors is a huge deal. You are admitting that people have found your behavior to be offensive and unwelcome, yet it is not your intent to offend or hurt anyone, but simply to help the team improve.

In such situations, the person often is surprised or reactive in the moment when that behavior comes up. If someone is extremely straightforward and accused of being blunt, the person who is guilty of this would benefit from examples of it. By admitting that this is a challenge for you, you have deescalated the fact that it may surprise somebody that this behavior comes out, and it reduces the risk that someone's feelings are hurt. They are aware that *you* are aware. And now they appreciate that you have awareness of it. Let them know it may happen. And there is no longer a huge negative response out of surprise, or out of defensiveness, if something happens that they do not agree with, and this behavior offends in any way.

The second part is that, from a perspective of humility and openness, you have given others permission to let you know if in fact you are engaging in that behavior. The good news is that most offenses are *not* intentional. This will be great learning for a teammate if the team can communicate in a helpful manner and agree to come alongside someone who has admitted they have displayed an unfavorable trait or behavior.

My Two Favorite Team Words: I Will

Another aspect of integrity is simply being a person of your word, being authentic and genuine about what you are willing to accomplish. That does not mean saying yes to everything, but it does mean that you are forthright, honest, and formidable about what you are and are not willing to do. People who strive diligently toward being a person of their word and holding themselves accountable to being able to meet the standard of "doing what I said I would do" are often found to be of high integrity. I surround myself with people who say, "I will." There are many difficult and uncomfortable tasks within any organization and team. But when someone says, "I will take out the trash," or "I will play center in the absence of our big man" (*Magic Johnson*), or the team member who sacrifices their own role to aid the team in a needed way, that's when the coach says, "I'll take 10 more players just like the Johnson kid!"

I pay remarkably close attention to the team members who duck out, make excuses, and generally have an unwillingness to do anything that is not clearly defined as *their role*. Doing a little extra and being a team member means helping where you can and serving others. As my friend Kevin Santiago loves to say, "It's not about you." We have learned we need each person's strength to culminate in the power of *us*.

Key Takeaways

- High standards are the only acceptable benchmark.
- Staying at the top when the competition seeks to knock you off highlights the need for continuous excellence and resilience.
- Keep the team aligned and swiftly address members who may be out of alignment.
- Individual standards start with integrity and being conditioned morally, mentally, physically, and emotionally.
- The power of a team is the culmination of individual efforts creating a stronger and more resilient collective "us."

- The mindset of an effective team member signifies commitment and an initiative-taking attitude toward the organization's goals.

The Pain Exchange

Being excellent is a choice that is made daily. I aim for 1% better every day. I am not staying the same. I get better or worse each day.

- Spend at least 10–15 minutes daily reading something uplifting and that will ground your moral compass.
- Reading suggestions: the Bible, Jesus Calling, leadership, inspirational biography, self-development, or similar. Commit to this 10–15-minute reading session within the first two hours of your day.

Advanced Pain Exchange

1. Begin your day with a 10-10-10:

   10 minutes of inspirational or development reading

   10 minutes of meditation

   10 minutes of journaling

2. Pick up *The Oak Journal* (www.oakjournal.com, promo code: WFAW) and start tracking your life's work on the daily and get intentional about achieving your goals! (See the section "Gratitude" in Chapter 6 for more about this.)

6

Mindset: Fail Faster and WTF (Willing to Fail)

ONE OF THE first requirements for me with organizations I'm working with is that we replace some commonly used words, beginning with the word "problem." I hear "we have big problems" in a lot of organizations. The word is deflating and influences teams' attitudes and outlooks. The reaction to the word is visceral: eye rolling, slumping shoulders, poor body language, and clenched jaws, to name a few. Replacing the word "problem" with "challenge" engages a mindset shift in how we respond emotionally, and sometimes even physically.

Words (and Thoughts) Matter

As we see people work through these values, self-talk becomes an absolute critical part of your journey of excellence. I love the Henry Ford quote "If you think you can, or you think you can't, you're right." As a child I often read the book *The Little Engine That Could*. I recall starting to tell myself positive things as I went to high school, knowing that one of my biggest adversaries was the voice inside my head, making excuses, blaming others, urging me to quit hard things, and ignoring data. So my loser behaviors could easily come out because my internal voice was supporting those standards, and it was not working for me, and may have even been working against me. Imagine, me versus me, and my internal self is winning! If your internal voice is holding you back and producing negative behaviors or results, you must start there to turn it around.

Friend Talk

Ann Gaffigan, US Steeplechase Record Holder; New Balance Pro Athlete; Women in Tech Leader; COO, United Way of Greater Kansas City

Ann is a poster child example of a phenomenal athlete who maximized her ability, and then transitioned from sport to her career. Once an Olympic hopeful and owning the American Steeplechase record (2004), she now leads teams in technology. She brings her many learnings from her time on the track to leading teams as a chief technology officer for multiple brands! Her passion for leading even moved the needle on the Olympic Committee when they added Steeplechase to the Olympic docket in 2008.

I had great anticipation to have an American record holder on *Winners Find a Way*. Ann did not disappoint!

TRENT: RUNNING CAN BE A LONELY SPORT, AND IT IS OFTEN NOTED AS ONE OF THE MOST GRUELING AND PAINFUL, BOTH PHYSICALLY AND MENTALLY. WITH LOTS OF TIME TO THINK, WHAT WAS YOUR STRATEGY TO GET YOUR MINDSET RIGHT?

Ann: I focused on just this day. Let's start over if you have a good race today, let's be happy today. And let's not think about where you thought you would be three years ago and just go from there. And it worked, it really worked.

"Talk to yourself the way your best friend would talk to you."
– Ann Gaffigan

HAVING PEAKED LATE IN YOUR COLLEGIATE CAREER AT
NEBRASKA, WHAT WAS THE BREAKTHROUGH FOR YOU?

I largely did not have a successful collegiate career. Until the
NCAA championships my senior year, I was average and, in
some cases, below average. And so, when I went into my senior year, I had yet to reach any of the goals that I had assumed
I would achieve. I had set out to achieve certain school records,
winning the Big 12 meet—it was Big 12 still when I was in
college at Nebraska—the NCAA championships, or even all-
American; I hadn't even qualified for the NCAA championships yet going into my senior year, much less be considered an
all-American. And I certainly wasn't near qualifying for the
2004 Olympic trials, much less considered a favorite to make
the US Olympic team.

When I went into that final senior season, it was just a
crisis in my head. Who am I? Because all my life, I'd grown
up to where I thought I was this amazing athlete who would
accomplish all these things. And here I was, just really, really
struggling. And I just thought to myself, "You know what,
I want to look back on this year and say that I did everything I could."

ONCE YOU MADE THE SHIFT IN YOUR MIND TO LEAVE IT ALL
ON THE TRACK, AND HOW DO YOU GET YOUR MINDSET RIGHT
TO BALANCE IT ALL?

You have to make sure that you're not letting yourself get over-
whelmed and that you're also reacting to everything appropri-
ately. Probably just my own demons, but I used to be so hard
on myself and just kind of condescending and mean in my
head. And I feel like I took that energy and turned it around to
fight for me instead of against me.

(continued)

(*continued*)

WHAT WOULD YOU TELL SOMEONE STARTING THEIR JOURNEY
TO BE THEIR BEST SELF, ATHLETE, AND CONTRIBUTOR?

I think your best self is in there; it is not an accident. And if
you don't feel that, then you have to do the work to find him
or her and to bring that person to the day instead of whatever
you're getting in the moment, and I think what people miss is
that they are entirely in control of that. They can make a decision as to how they want to talk to themselves, how they want
to approach the day. They can figure out the proper triggers for
themselves, whether that is getting up and exercising or medi-
tating or listening to certain types of music. My mood, I found,
I can really change with music. And so that is a great thing!
Then if you have your playlist or your genre that is your go-to
list to get you in the right mindset, then you know that about
yourself. So I think people miss how much they are in control
of their own life and how they feel about it.

I HAVE HEARD YOU USE THE TERM "WAYFINDER." CAN
YOU EXPLAIN WHAT THIS MEANS?

I've heard it referred to as wayfinding, where instead of saying, "I want to get here. Here's where I am and I'm going to
get there," you're just taking one milestone at a time and
figuring out how that changes your direction of where you're
going based on all the new information and experience
that you have.

> *"You may end up here. You may end up there. Who knows?
> But why limit yourself to this destination if it ends up not being
> the right one for you?"*
>
> – Ann Gaffigan

Wayfinder

I love this so much I think I'll have T-shirts made up for "Way-finder"! Through the years I've witnessed many goal setters become so fixed on the destination that they don't enjoy the journey at all, and then they find out the destination was *not* where they wanted to be. That is a rough moment filled with a lot of confusion and distress over all the efforts made to get to the wrong place.

WTF and Fail Faster

In Brian Scudamore's book *WTF (Willing to Fail)*, he discusses the theory that so few people are willing to take the risk and be okay underperforming for an abbreviated period to learn what is required to be able to master and win. *Fail Fast, Fail Often: How Losing Can Help You Win* by John D. Krumboltz and Ryan Babineaux is another book that addresses this concept of risk and hyper-learning.

I have developed an affinity for failing. I get energized when things are not going well. I find that most people and teams are complacent when winning and especially when they have a consistent level of success. But failing brings pain and discomfort. The organization and its people are ready and willing to look at that failure and generally want to win, and they really want to eliminate the discomfort and pain. An athlete has been trained to spring into action, to tackle the challenges head on and adjust. My excitement is in anticipation of the changes the team will make that will ultimately make them better as an organization by resolving a sizeable challenge. Growth and development are inevitable—that gets me jazzed up!

Gratitude

Gratitude in our hearts that is genuine is a prerequisite for getting our mindset right. I'm a huge fan of a daily planner called *The Oak Journal*. One of the key items is starting your day with gratitude for three things in your life. It can involve anything.

If I start the morning with 10 minutes of inspirational reading and take three to five minutes to plan my day, and then sprinkle the mindset of abundance through gratitude, it sets me up for whatever the day brings. I believe we live in the best country in the world. I know I'm biased, but I've traveled to close to 40 other countries and learned a great deal. Our freedoms and economic opportunities dwarf many other countries and make it special. We should never lose sight of that.

I like to take the 10,000-foot view of things that have me challenged or are challenging me to stay positive. If you have ever been up in a plane, 10,000 feet is a very cool view. You can still see major landmarks, recognizable topography, distinct buildings, and properties, and can even make out cars and buses on the road. Yet you won't see a small accident between two cars that look like ants! The issues remain and are real, but the perspective is vastly different.

Self-Talk and Intellectual Humility

Marty Strong, Author, *Be Nimble, Be Visionary* and nine novels under a pen name; Navy SEAL; Black Belt, Six Sigma; two-time cancer survivor

Marty was recommended to me by a friend, who told me about his many accomplishments. I love talking to Navy SEALs; they have a mindset trained above all, and share the best stories. Marty has wrangled his storytelling into nine books under his pen name that are fabulous fiction reading. I highly recommend them.

Marty transferred his extensive military experience and training to lead business development and sales teams, and become a CEO of a management group as well as a healthcare company.

I started our *Winners Find a Way* show by setting a base for where Marty had been, and how it shaped his current views.

(*Author's note: The 24-week BUD/S (Basic Underwater Demolition/SEAL) training is considered extremely difficult to pass, with an attrition rate between 70% and 85% per class. Anyone can voluntarily quit the program at any time by opting out and walking over to the middle of the compound and ringing the bell. The suffering ends immediately. Or does it?*)

TRENT: WHEN YOU WERE GOING THROUGH BUD/S, THINGS WERE DIFFERENT IN THE SEALs. EXPLAIN HOW THIS PROGRESSED FROM A MINDSET STANDPOINT.

Marty: Regarding my self-talk on entering the SEALs, I call those "voices in your head," and I will tell you the voices in my head were pretty much saying, "Okay, come to grips. *This is reality.*"

The grief and challenge of transitioning, after ringing the bell for any reason, was what I went through because when you ring the bell, the officers would put you in a truck and take you across to all the ships and stick you on a ship and you start painting—grunt work—and they don't care about your psychology. When I came back as an instructor eight years later, [the trainers] were smarter. So if guys rang the bell at different points, they'd send them to deep-sea diving school or bomb disposal because they were smart. They were sharp guys, so that was a much better way to transition top talent.

WHAT DO YOU THINK WAS KEY IN YOUR TRAINING FOR MINDSET?

You strip out all your accolades and all your failures in a clear mind, then you have intellectual curiosity, sucking everything in around you—360-degree situational awareness, with whatever you're doing.

(*continued*)

(*continued*)

WHAT ARE SOME OF THE LEARNINGS THAT YOU HAD ALONG THE WAY TO TRANSITION FROM THE SEALS TO BUSINESS?

Step one, be humble. Then listen to people to whom you don't normally listen. Seek information, insights from weird places. And then the third step is intellectual creativity. Because you can be intellectually creative and reshape what your world is or what your business looks like if you have taken those other two steps. But the key one is the humility one. And if you haven't been humiliated, it's a hard thing to get to. So you've got to practice it a little bit by putting yourself out there.

WHAT WAS ONE OF YOUR KEY INSIGHTS INTO SOMEONE'S MINDSET THAT YOU LEARNED ALONG THE WAY?

We used to read eyes all the time as BUD/S instructors. We could tell, and we could write down, exactly who was going to quit. You could see it in their eyes. And in Viktor Frankl's *Man's Search for Meaning*, he is talking about his experience in the German death camps, and he says it exactly, almost word for word. Within a couple of hours, he saw people shut down. And that was it. He knew they were done. You can see it in their eyes, and you could try to drag them back from that. But that was a rarity.

> *"But there's a point when they get to where they believe what they're hearing. Instead of being the voice in their head, they are listening to the voices in their head. But I think you have to get out of your comfort zone. And the more you do it, the more you get used to the process you must have. I teach and talk about a little intellectual humility as the basis."*
> *— Marty Strong*

The Book of Proverbs written by King Solomon—the wisest, wealthiest, and most powerful man in history—is often referred to as the Book of Wisdom. The fourth chapter talks about staying on the path and being leery of the ways of the wicked and deep darkness. This hits for me at verse 23: "Above all else, guard your heart, for everything you do flows from it." Most folks think mindset is headspace and sometimes feels like "head trash." But let's get back to the root cause—our thoughts flow from our hearts. Get your heart right "above all else . . . for everything you do flows from it." And this includes your words, thoughts, and that inner voice in your mind.

If we are taking trash in, trash must go out. This shows up in several ways and manifests itself in bad attitudes, disrespect, and many other poor behaviors. But we are a civil society and we do not say outwardly every thought that comes to our minds. That is likely a good thing. Though we have millions of thoughts, we are still shaped by this internal voice. So is that voice saying positive things to you? Is it your biggest advocate and a good friend?

Here is one question I ask a lot of folks: Do you allow people to speak to you with disrespect and contempt, or do you expect others to speak to you in a manner of etiquette and respect? We don't care for being disrespected or talked down too. So if you won't allow others to do that, why would you allow *you* to do it to yourself?

We are our own harshest critic, and it is painful not to meet or exceed our own expectations for ourselves. We have standards, intentions, and goals. We work diligently toward those things all the time, though a setback in the process or journey can yield a firestorm internally. Hope is *not* a strategy. We keep grace in our hearts for others, but sometimes will not allow ourselves to have any. That's bonkers!

Poor self-talk comes from a heart that has not been protected and guarded, and it is fueled by comparison, envy, mismatched results, jealousy, dislike/hate, contempt, excuses, blame, willful ignorance, idolatry, neglect, and negative influences from those around you.

This last area is tough as it is often stated that we become a version of the five people we are around the most. Have you ever considered those folks closest to you and how their self-talk is going? You should remove yourself from any negative influence as soon as possible so there is no longer a regular negative impact on you. This is challenging when those people are part of your family dynamic.

Vision and Breathing

In the 1980s, more athletes were tapping into visualization work. I envisioned playing well and at a superior level to even my current skills to get in the mindset of the speed of the game and flow. Countless athletes have had significant success by having regular sessions prior to practicing or competing in their given sport. It is a fabulous mental exercise to prepare the body too. There was a study of average players shooting free throws for practice with three groups to measure. One was the group that took their shots and then did nothing for four weeks. The second group was not allowed to practice shooting but sat down each day and visualized making the free throws for 20 minutes. The third group practiced their shots each day for the four weeks. Not surprisingly, the third group improved the most. Accordingly, the group that did nothing was not any better after the four weeks. The surprise was the second group that only visualized the shots. They improved almost as much as the group that practiced daily.

Breathing techniques are also value-added. I recently went through different breathing techniques as I prepared to take the stage for my TEDx Talk in Utah. Fatigue, nerves, and anxiety were waging war internally. I felt this for years in certain situations, most often when in the batter's box in a close game. The deep-breathing techniques of bringing oxygen in through your nose and filtering that air with your nose hairs to maximize oxidation to the blood is important. Learning breathing techniques can be a massive advantage to allowing your mindset to stay focused on the tasks at hand, instead of giving into the body's physiological response.

During a closely contested game late in the 2002 World Series, Angels' outfielder Garrett Anderson was at the plate. The crowd was going wild and yelling at the top of their lungs. The pressure was palpable to me as a strength and conditioning coach knowing all the preparation leading to these moments. But now I was nothing more than a not-so-cool-and-calm observer. And then, between pitches, Garret took a step out of the box leaning on his heels and *yawned!* I was outraged internally. I wanted to ask him if he was bored. This was one of the biggest moments in the Angels journey to the World Championship . . . and our star was yawning! Then he hit a double. Later I learned that yawning gives a massive shot of oxygen to the body and helps in relaxing it, flooding the critical muscles and organs with oxygenated blood. *Brilliant!*

A Change in Response Is a Change in Outcome

This brings us to the next key element in this journey: how do we deal with challenges? I like the E + R = O theory of father and son thought leaders Tim and Brian Kight:

An **Event** happens, we make a **Response**, and then there is an **Outcome**.

We likely don't get to control the event that happens, and the *only way* there is going to be a different outcome is through our response. So the theory says that our response becomes the big part of the equation where we have the most impact on the outcome.

It seems like a simple formula, yet leaders, team members, and people in general respond horribly to events each day and they're getting poor outcomes because of it—turnover, losses, closed accounts, job loss. Whatever it is, the outcomes are not what people want them to be. If we do not recognize our response to the matter, we're missing a key element of this journey because the best in the world respond very well to challenges (events). And they are ready to pivot and adapt and respond in a positive way, creating better outcomes. Often the event or the perceived risk creates fear. And most folks do not respond well to fear!

I have evaluated this theory with my own spouse as our disagreements have had recurring patterns for years. We met when we were 16 and 15 years old and have been married over 29 years. Our high school style of debate and reasoning (or lack thereof) remained evident and emotionally driven. So though most would consider us both above-average EQ-rated, our patterns were to revert to defensiveness and emotional outbursts—not great. What I saw was how effective it was when both of us changed our "standard" response and came at things with calmness and patience. We were much more likely to produce a positive outcome. Crazy, right!?

Fear What and Why Fear
Ken Mannie, 25-year Head Strength and Conditioning Coach, Michigan State University

Ken was my first mentor when I left my home state of Michigan at the ripe old age of 20. I headed to the University of Toledo, and Ken was the university's head strength and conditioning coach for all the athletes.

I had an affinity for training since I was in seventh grade working out with one of my older brothers, Trev. It didn't hurt that most of my class work at UT was directly across from the weight room entrance and Ken's office. I was a regular attendee in the athletes' weight room and always "going the extra mile" to compete at the Division I level.

Ken liked me immediately. Coaches love athletes who are willing to work, listen, and then execute, and are willing to make the necessary sacrifices to become elite. Ken has been an inspiration for my career and one of my most admired friends. He makes everyone around him better. He is laser focused and has no time for inefficiency. He also lives out exactly what he is asking all of us to do. He has been in phenomenal shape his entire career and life.

I was used to sitting down with Ken to "pick his brain." He always obliged and entertained all my questions and theories.

TRENT: I HAVE FELT FEAR MOST OF MY LIFE, AND I BELIEVE MOST HIGH ACHIEVERS RECOGNIZE IT, BUT WHAT WOULD BE YOUR APPROACH TO TAKING IT ON?

Ken: To overcome fear, you must understand *what* you are afraid of and *why* you are afraid of it. Use that information to develop tools, set goals, and create standards to overcome that fear every single day.

WHAT IS YOUR APPROACH TO GOAL SETTING AND PERSONAL DEVELOPMENT?

There is no finish line in life. You just keep going, improving, and working toward the goals that you want to achieve. Overachieve and go the extra mile when you can. Each person brings a unique perspective and value to a team. Being satisfied will get you in a comfort zone.

- "This day for that day." Set the goal out one year, that day. Work each day, *this* day, to be the best you can, and then be the best you can each of the 364 days until *that* day. Goal attained!
- Then reset for the next goal. Make your timelines your own.
- Develop and understand the processes that worked along the way.

EXPLAIN YOUR RIDE-OR-DIE VIEW ON PERSONAL RESPONSIBILITY.

Everything you do matters, so you must ask yourself if you are willing to put your name on something. Are you willing to fully commit your time, efforts, and talents? Your actions can reflect either negatively or positively on everything you are involved with.

"Do not just do a drive-by on the extra mile; build your house on it!"

– *Ken Mannie*

I love the idea that Coach Mannie is asking us all to *understand* better what we are afraid of, and lean into it, as opposed to running from it. We all fear things and we have a fight-or-flight response. I do not know if we necessarily must choose to fight, but the flight response to fear often does not produce the result we want. In the case of acute (short-term) fear in a dire situation such as a fire, get out of there—flight is best! But chronic (long-term) fear requires a fight response. Go toe-to-toe. Understanding this and learning from our fear is critical, and I do believe fear can be an exceptionally good teacher. But I take the fear I feel in a situation and use it to gain information, develop tools, set goals, and create standards to overcome, just as Coach Mannie instructed.

To his point, there is no finish line on this journey. We learn that we probably are going to have to change our process to achieve our goals. And that's okay. If we develop a better process, we don't just achieve our one goal, but we achieve that goal (and others) again and again and again.

I love that Coach Mannie promotes going the "extra mile," and that a person going beyond the minimum standard is so important because being satisfied is a death march to being average. Coach Mannie's statement on this journey is that most goals are set ahead of us to a measurable number of days.

As I recall, I made my goals of becoming a college scholarship athlete at an early age, and I started tracking it when I was a first-year student in high school. So that goal wouldn't become a reality for me for more than three years, meaning that I would have well over 1,000 *this* days when I would have to prepare and work with focus and intent for *that* day to happen.

We either get better or we get worse each day. We do not stay the same. I'm asking myself this question all the time: What can I do this day to move just a little bit closer to that day when my goal is met and I stand on the podium, or I receive the degree, or I get the job (whatever that day is for you)?

Shorten the time to get to that day by completing at least three valuable tasks for each day. So it may not take four years to accomplish that degree; maybe you do it in three years. You become focused every day on the things that should and must be done, plus taking action to complete those items.

The Shampoo Treatment

Once I get to *that* day, I take a moment to celebrate. I have trained my mind to achieve, and the reward reinforces in my mind the training and keeps me focused on the next journey. Then my next move is to reset for my next *that* day. What is next for me? What is the next thing I want?

And I'm starting to prioritize, even during my current journey. What will be the next thing that I will look to accomplish? And if the next thing is going to take 100 days, I have 99 *this* days to get to *that* day.

It may be short, it may be long, but what am I doing on this day for that day? Develop and understand the processes that worked along the way and utilize the *shampoo treatment*: wash, rinse, repeat. Once you've developed a great process, continue that process. Rinse that process out, make sure it is still a winner, go over it, and then repeat that process again. Great organizations and teams have great processes. You must have your mind right and focused to be your best.

The Ford Company was known early on for their process. They perfected how to establish an assembly line and a process to build vehicles. This changed the very fabric of planning and transportation in our country, as well as creating millions and millions of jobs for roads, signs, building construction, and more. Henry Ford was a consistent proponent of having his mindset in the right place and understood the power of our self-talk.

The Journey of Excellence Summary

Think of a painting or fabulous piece of art. The artist signs their work, literally "putting their name on it." In whatever ways you can fully commit to and be the best you can be at—do it with all your effort. Put your name on it and reap the rewards!

Our willingness to put our name on our efforts and work, along with the fortitude and sacrifice to take the acute pain of discipline, while fully committing our time, focus, and talents so that our consistent actions will reflect positively on everything we're involved with—that is the journey to excellence.

Key Takeaways

- Embrace failure and be open to taking risks and learning from mistakes.
- Comfort is the enemy of greatness and failure accelerates learning.
- Talk to yourself as you would to a good friend.
- Be mindful of your commitment and goals, then approach the challenges with a sense of purpose and dedication.
- Stay intellectually curious and open minded with a desire for humility and continuous learning.
- Be a wayfinder, navigating the journey without rigid expectations.
- Guard your heart, as all thoughts, words, and actions flow from it.
- Overcome fears utilizing breathing and visualization techniques.
- Approach each day with mental readiness.
- Deliver more than is expected and own your efforts.

The Pain Exchange

When thinking about your next big goal, ask yourself what you are dreaming about. Our dreams and what wakes us up at night are the important things on our mind. Get them aligned with your expertise and vision to where you see your life and journey headed.

Choose your next goal and determine the deadline for the goal: or *that* day! Then determine how many *this* days you will have to reach your goal.

Build your plan of attack on the goal by determining a breakdown of 90 days, or 3 months, increments for whatever is a reasonable period to achieve your goal.

For ease on this, choose a goal with a deadline of three years or less.

You will have no more than 12 quarters, or twelve 90-day periods, to create the value you need to achieve your goal. If one year, four quarters. For two years, eight quarters.

The stepped areas of achievement will be broken down by quarter as a mini goal. We will have 89 *this* days for *that* day on each stepped mini-goal, and 365, 730, or 1,095 days depending on *that* full big goal.

Get an accountability partner/guide/coach. The best in the world have support teams around them—why wouldn't you if you are going for something big!?

7

The Importance of Routine, Focus, and Training for Adaptability

The Power of the Three Ps

1. PLAN

Putting a winning game plan together is not every athlete's strength. Most athletes are given the plan and taught what each of them needs to do so that the team accomplishes the plan together. Most athletes have never been on the inside to really learn the how, what, and why of what an organization is going for.

Hire a Catcher Approximately 50% of the managers today in MLB are former catchers. They are consistently held in the role of field general and communicator to the rest of the team. They must have a comprehensive approach and knowledge of all that the coaches are looking to pass on to critical personnel. Catchers will sit in on meetings with coaches and staff, the pitching coach, the hitting coach, a team meeting, and a defensive coach. No one single player communicates more to the staff than a catcher. He becomes the go-between with the staff and the field personnel who must execute the plan. I would consider him a facilitator and integrator. I believe this is the reason that so many baseball catchers become managers and leaders.

In addition to all the staff communications and off-field responsibilities, the catcher must maintain their own physical skills of catching, throwing, hitting, and running, while maintaining an elevated level of emotional intelligence and control. An emotional outburst or poor relationship with an umpire is detrimental and affects the whole team in some capacity. Poise is key for catchers to be successful, and they become fabulous integrators.

Game plans have a few features: an overarching summary of the plan to win and a strategy to accomplish it and meet the end goal, and a number of key metrics, often referred to as KPIs (key performance indicators) that will assign measurements to training, actions, timelines, and alignment to achieve the overall goal.

Focused Game Planning   Leadership teams spend long hours, energy, and efforts to put strategic plans together. They do not work all the time, and that is fine. Not ideal, but sometimes we're learning what doesn't work, and we can pivot. The idea of having details and measurements, plus tracking, becomes important to our ability to communicate and have visibility around our execution and learn what is working and what may not be.

Review the Tapes   Athletes must go back to see if they execute on what they were asked to do, and this part of leadership feels second nature. Get feedback and make a few adjustments! No problem. Where I see people getting in trouble is being unwilling to review what happened and ignore the data that is right in front of them. Guessing, hoping, and ignoring will not get your team where you want to go.

The Fourth-Quarter Program

David Gregory, Former College Football Player; NFL Agent;
Lobbyist; Lawyer; Influencer's Parent

David is an attorney and spent years in the government space
as a lobbyist. He started as a client, developing the firm for
maximum value, and then sold his position and transitioned
into being an NFL agent. As a former college football player,
and with his background in the law, this made perfect sense.

David and I met through a mutual friend. He joined *Winners Find a Way* near the time the NCAA was going to change
the structure for Name, Image, and Likeness (NIL).

TRENT: AS A LONG-TIME MICHIGAN STATE UNIVERSITY FAN,
YOU FOLLOWED COACH SABAN CLOSELY, AND BECAUSE
HE WORKED ALONGSIDE YOUR FORMER COACH, BUCK NYSTROM.
WHAT IS YOUR STANCE ON COACH SABAN AS A LEADER?

David: Well, number one, I'm different than most. I grew up
with Michigan State. Most Michigan State fans hate Nick
Saban. I just never did.

Nick Saban was the young defensive back coach and Buck
Nystrom was an established coach. Coach Saban openly credits Buck; he says, "I got my fourth-quarter conditioning program, which isn't just conditioning. There are a lot of values
embedded in it and a lot of approaches embedded in it. That is
Buck Nystrom's fourth-quarter program that he invented. And
I took it from him when I went to the pros, I took it to Michigan State, LSU, Alabama, and that's been one of the founda-
tions of the program ever since." So I always followed him
from that aspect because I knew he ran the fourth-quarter conditioning program. I knew that my coach had invented it.

(continued)

(*continued*)

I know that I'd been through that program, at least a version of it, in my own college days.

IF YOU COULD GIVE SOME ADVICE TO ATHLETES WHO ARE EITHER TRANSITIONING FROM SPORT TO BUSINESS, OR LIFE NOW, WHAT IS THE ONE SUPERPOWER YOU THINK IS MOST IMPORTANT?

"I just think the ability to grind through things, and it's such a cliché, but take the game one play at a time. I mean, the game is played one play at a time. It is not played one quarter at a time. Life is the same."

— David Gregory

---

2. PROCESS

Once a great game plan is in place, we must figure out *how* we are going to get it done. I'm good on teams not knowing how to do this, which seems counterintuitive. A good plan should have clear process, but sometimes it's not there yet. When you have top players who have been coached to figure out better processes and procedures every year by exceptionally good game planners and play at the highest levels where others are also extremely good at figuring out process, then you are ahead of most. Your team has hyper-learned by reviewing the tapes on what worked, and they take note of what the opposing team did, what they learned, and what may have been used effectively against them.

Formulas for Winning   Athletes have been taught for years to follow process and learn the system, which is ultimately a formula. Athletes go through tons of different systems and formulas and learn effectiveness and ineffectiveness along the way. Unfortunately, most athletes spend much of their time playing in ineffective formulas that do not produce the result that ultimately the organization plans for. There are many reasons why the formulas fail. The athletes are regularly strategizing and assessing these formulas and adjusting them. They get exceptionally good at seeing patterns in those formulas and learning from their opponents and fellow teammates on adjustments they can make to create a winning formula!

Holistic Approach   Most organizations take a strategic approach to their many challenges and spend little time on their winning formulas. I like to look at holistic strategies having no less than six key qualities and often focusing on eight areas of productivity necessary to have a winning strategy and be able to execute that strategy for a winning formula. Now when I investigate organizations, most omit key areas that can significantly reduce the ability to develop a winning formula. If you don't have someone on the team who has experience, we look for an experienced person to assist, as they can see several diverse ways an organization can fail.

Regimented Routines
Scott Spiezio, MLB player, As, Angels, Mariners, and Cardinals (retired); Youth Baseball Instructor; Professional Speaker

I had the blessing of coaching Scott for about four years in Anaheim when we were both with the Angels and enjoyed winning a World Series together. Scott had one of the best post-seasons of all time in 2002, yet he was not a superstar at that time. Scott was committed to consistent daily action to develop his disciplined routines for success.

(continued)

(*continued*)

Be sure to look up the epic battle Scott had with ace reliever Felix Rodriguez in Game 6 of the 2002 World Series. His three-run home run in the seventh inning on an eight-pitch at bat is the stuff of legends, a war where he proclaimed victory! The momentum itself catapulted our entire team to believe in what is possible. And in a 1980 USA Hockey Miracle–like string of comebacks, the Angels claimed victory in the 2002 World Championship.

Scott joined one of our first episodes of *Winners Find a Way*. It was a tell-all of what had happened to this former hero and champion in getting on the other side of a 10-year battle with drugs and alcohol. In our full interview, Scott speaks about his early days of training with his father, who also played in the major leagues. In fact, Scott and his father, Ed, are the only father-son combination to have both won a World Series, and the Spiezios also did it for the same franchise, as Scott won the World Series Championship with the St. Louis Cardinals in 2006, and his father in 1968, both beating the Detroit Tigers, oddly enough.

Scott's success wasn't a fluke. It would not have happened without his discipline and training, which produced a regimented workload and routines that he and his father established at an early age, with Ed taking his learnings from the drills of major leaguers and applying the practices with Scott. With the daily work that Scott was willing to commit to, it is not by chance that he had the success he did. His preparation levels were far beyond what most kids are doing today, to get to the next level. Four to eight hours of training per day was common on top of his schoolwork and normal practice schedules.

TRENT: WHAT FINALLY BROUGHT YOU OUT OF THIS HORRIFIC CYCLE AND TO NOW FIVE-PLUS YEARS OF SOBRIETY (ABOUT ONE AND A HALF YEARS AT THE TIME OF THE EPISODE).

Scott: You know it's starting with just moving one stick, just doing one thing, and digging yourself out of that. I didn't know it at the time, but I was putting on the armor of God and I did not even realize it. It was just my way. Instead of going to the bars and hanging out with the guys, I would go and read my Bible, then play my guitar a little bit.

I felt I was failing as a father and I basically started crying when confronted with my family I had lost, and I asked my kids—I had all three (at that time) of them around me, I'm like, "Would it just be better if I wasn't involved in your life?" They all started crying and said, "No, no, we love you." And my oldest son said, "It's never too late, Dad, it's never too late." It just hit me. It is never too late and that was the start of me starting to get back on track.

I basically stopped justifying my sins. I stopped surrounding myself with people that didn't have the best influence on me.

WALK ME THROUGH THE NIGHT YOUR ENTIRE CAREER AND LIFE CHANGED ON OCTOBER 26, 2002. THIS HOME RUN WILL FOREVER BE IN MAJOR LEAGUE BASEBALL HISTORY AS ONE OF THE BEST AFTER AN EIGHT-PITCH BATTLE OF AN AT-BAT WITH ONE OF THE BEST, FELIX RODRIGUEZ. WHAT WAS YOUR MENTALITY GOING INTO THE AT-BAT, AND WAS THIS WHAT MADE YOU SO SUCCESSFUL DURING ALL YOUR PLAYOFF EFFORTS?

My whole mentality was just trying to drive the ball in the gap. I am telling myself, don't try to do too much. I wasn't thinking of a home run. I was basically trying to get something middle and go and get a run on the board. And finally on the eighth pitch, three balls, two strikes, he threw it down and in and I got just enough of it to get it out. And I was praying on the way to first base, Lord, please push this one out.

(continued)

(*continued*)

And as far as I'd say the two things that separated me were my work ethic and preparation, both physically and mentally, which led to mental toughness.

AS A MAN WHO HAS BEEN THROUGH SOME OF THE MOST INTENSE CHALLENGES PEOPLE FACE, WHAT WOULD YOU TELL PEOPLE WHO ARE GOING THROUGH TRIALS AND MAY BE STUCK TODAY AND LOOKING FOR WISDOM FROM SOMEONE THAT HAS BEEN THERE?

Well, you just got to have that "never give up" mentality. It's easy to get buried by all the weight of everything, you know, your addiction, your broken relationships, and the guilt of doing everything. And first you have to stop listening to naysayers, get away from the people telling you that you are worthless. Get away from them. Start reading the Word. So the devil is not throwing his fiery darts at you, and saying, "You're worthless, you're not worthy of Jesus's salvation." I had to stop listening to that and surrounding myself with better people, reading the Word, and just go out and start moving sticks, literally.

I HAVE OFTEN SAID WE OFTEN LEARN BEST FROM OUR FAILURES, AND WE CAN GET COMPLACENT WITH SUCCESS. WHAT WOULD YOU TELL SOMEONE ABOUT LEARNING FROM FAILURE?

Overcoming failure is huge. But learning from your mistakes is huge, too. You see these billionaires, a lot of them have failed multiple times and went bankrupt at least once. And in any part of life, learning from failure—me going through what I went through—I've learned so much more empathy, and more love. I wouldn't be the person I am today if I didn't fail. And I failed miserably in a lot of ways. This is especially true with addiction, and as a father. Now I've learned from those mistakes, and I am doing everything I can to correct those mistakes.

When you are at the bottom, you see what is important, and you prioritize. And as for baseball, there were many times where I might get a strike out on a backdoor slider or something. And so the next time up to bat, I make the adjustment. I learned from what pitchers are doing to me. And the next time you try to do that again, I'm hitting the ball down the left field line.

WAS THERE SOMETHING YOU COULD DO AS A TRIGGER OR REMINDER WHEN THINGS WERE NOT GOING WELL TO GET YOU BACK TO YOUR FOCUS AND ALIGNED WITH YOUR TASK AT HAND AND GOALS?

I would have clear keys during the game, where I would wipe my bat off or wipe the ground. And that would get rid of all negative thoughts about any mistake I made, whether it be an error or swinging on a bad pitch. And I could go right back in my focus. But then after the game on the drive home, I was saying to myself, "I hope that you learn from them." And replaying them in my mind the way I wanted. And then I would reinforce with successful times—successful moments that produced successful plays. I would replay those over and over with many, many highlight reels for myself, to reinforce those positive outcomes.

3. PRODUCTIVITY

Show me definitions of what productivity looks like. In the end, I'm focused on getting the desired result. Measurements often predicate what productivity will look like in our team. We will lean into strategies and communications that will indicate what KPIs are measured to clearly indicate what achievement will be measured by.

Clarity As organizations progress, they produce ways of simplification and prioritization that are required for their teams to know exactly how they can measure their success and all team members know what a valued contributor will be for the organization. They know their goals as well as a boss's expectations for their job, and what it looks like to exceed expectations.

I use Bloom Growth™ with my clients and in my businesses whenever we are discussing a comprehensive approach to our team and knowing that it is so critical that we execute and communicate on how we are attaining our goals and shoring up our process to make winning achievable repeatedly.

As we simplify and prioritize each team member's area of expertise and role in contributing to the greater impact of our organization, it's amazing to see people enjoy their work, value being a part of a winning team, enjoy interacting with fellow team members, value the feeling of accomplishment, and feel empowered as they help create impact together. Each member is a big part of a greater good moving together. Good teams are like that!

Little Things Matter

Tim Selgo, Athletic Director, Grand Valley State University; Assistant Vice President, Mammoth Sports Consulting; Author

Tim was my associate athletic director when I arrived at the University of Toledo. Tim was a former basketball star for the Rockets and was on his way to becoming the athletic director. But plans changed, and Tim headed off with his young family to Grand Rapids, Michigan, and Grand Valley State University as their athletic director. I think Tim fell in love with the state and the school. He had a massive impact, along with creating a winning culture.

I have always looked up to Tim as a mentor and a guy who certainly understood the athlete's journey through sport and then life afterwards. Tim joined *Winners Find a Way* as the first athletic director I interviewed.

TRENT: WE HAVE TALKED ABOUT THE "LITTLE THINGS" AND A LOT OF FOLKS SEE THIS AS MICROMANAGING. IN SPORTS, WE'RE TRAINED THAT THE LITTLE THINGS HAVE SIGNIFICANT IMPACT. WHAT IS YOUR STANCE?

"If you want to be successful, if you want to be a one-percenter, you've got to do the little things well. Little things matter in business, in life, and in sports, especially when no one is watching."

– Tim Selgo

TRENT: IF YOU KNEW SOMEONE GOING THROUGH TRIALS AND NEEDED TO GET A HOLD OF ONE ACTION THEY COULD TAKE RIGHT NOW, WHAT WOULD YOU TELL THEM?

Tim: I think one of the most important things you can do, especially when you're going through tough times, is to take the first minutes of the day and just spend them in quiet and think and meditate and pray in whatever way is your tradition or your creed. And with respect to all of them, I think if people do that, I think they'll have a better way of handling the crisis of the day, or the adversity of the day, or the ongoing problems.

THERE IS SO MUCH WRITTEN NOW ON EMOTIONAL INTELLI-GENCE (EQ). WHAT WOULD YOU RECOMMEND TO FOLKS?

You want to find success, find a way during adversity to main-tain emotional control. You make good decisions when your emotions are under control. And if you stop and think in your

(continued)

(*continued*)

lifetime when you have made the most mistakes, you probably got all charged up about something, good or bad, and you didn't keep your emotions under control. That is so important, I think, to finding a way, especially during adversity.

COACH WOODEN DEFINED SUCCESS THIS WAY: "SUCCESS IS PEACE OF MIND ATTAINED ONLY THROUGH SELF-SATISFACTION IN KNOWING YOU MADE THE EFFORT TO DO THE BEST OF WHICH YOU'RE CAPABLE." YOU AND I BOTH SHARE A LOVE FOR LIFE-LONG LEARNING, SO HOW DO YOU DEFINE SUCCESS?

The great plays by great players when the team needs it most does not just happen. It happens because that player has spent hours in the weight room, with the coaches, with his team, always pushing to be better when it does not matter, so he can perform when it does.

The Daily Grind

"How do you eat an elephant? One bite at a time."

– Desmond Tutu

Strategy and big-picture thinking are fun to spend time on and important. But if it cannot be executed, those sessions become a loss of time and effort.

I believe that games are won, championships are won, by winning each day. Top athletes get this. They come to work to be the best they can be on this day, knowing full well it is what they get to control. Yesterday is over, a past that cannot be changed. The future is hopeful and formidable but will never be a part of the production and process.

"Everyone wants to win the day of the game, but few are willing to prepare for it."

– Harvey Mackay

Athletes have spent years in training. Most did not start out as the best in their sport, but they committed to working daily to gain the edge they needed. Once training starts to yield results, athletes attribute the success to their daily habits. So if they got this far in a limited time to spend on all the areas needing improvement, they begin to carve out time for more intentional training, and not just in areas they excel at, but now they are learning areas of focus that need more attention in order for them to be better.

Two things are critical about the daily grind:

1. Your work is measured and monitored by people who can help you get to the next level, and preferably someone who is already there.

2. There is a discipline of deep commitment to this day and completing the big three things, and even more.

I like having an accountability partner, or a reporting structure with a respected person, because I do not want to let them down. Another key element is making your day manageable. If you must spend half your day managing your schedule, then I doubt you'll be effective.

Effectiveness and efficiency will win the day. Efficient learning and maximizing time and effort will yield remarkable results. Athletes understand this as they learn time management from being trained in top programs. Small gains in these areas tend to yield extraordinary results.

Athletes understand that it is difficult to compete at the highest levels. Time is a massive variable because we all get to determine what we do with it. "You can't make the club in the tub," is a common phrase uttered in athletic programs. In other words, if you are hurt and are limited in your ability to practice and get better today, others are passing you and taking your repetitions. This is extremely challenging for any athlete, and not likely where you want to be. Everyone starts with the same 168 hours each week, 24 hours each day. How do we do everything required of us to yield maximum impact?

"Fatigue makes cowards of us all!"

– U.S. Army General George S. Patton

Warning: I see people who choose to give up sleep and recovery as their first strategy to higher production. Don't! Most of us want to see results and some ignore the recovery and regeneration of our bodies that happens during rest. Overuse injuries are one of the most common career-ending factors. I recently saw a sign along the highway that said driving while tired is the equivalent of driving while intoxicated. When we are fatigued our reflexes are slower, and our brain is foggy and will not make the best decisions or have proper discernment. Our judgment is affected, and fatigue impairs us. When we are impaired, we are less confident, and when less confident, we feel weak. Cowards are weak. Balance is part of making your day great. Having proper sleep, rest, and recovery is essential for performing at your best.

Key Takeaways

- Take one day at a time.
- Review the tapes before you plan.
- Build a strategy with metrics everyone understands.
- Have a winning formula with a clear process.
- Empower the team to contribute with success measurements.
- Sweat the small stuff.
- Use your time with efficiency and effectiveness.

The Pain Exchange

Create your own structure of discipline. Putting a practice of discipline into your daily routine begins with you, and I want you to build confidence in extending your ability to be disciplined to something new.

Start the change immediately—today or tomorrow.

When I do ask someone to "add" something to their routines, I ask them to *eliminate* a mirrored item that is causing wasteful inefficiency for them personally, or for their team or family.

Recent examples for me include adding a gallon of water per day and eliminating any added sugars from my diet. I also have added four 15- to 30-minute sessions in my infrared sauna per week. I batch my sauna time with reading, catching up on learning, and studying for my moral conditioning through podcasts, videos, and audio books. This can be as small as adding one new discipline, such as an increase in water consumption, or an extra 30 minutes of sleep per day, and as large as hiring a coach to review your entire daily, weekly, and monthly activities to perform at your peak each day. This begins with a breakdown of start, stop, and continue.

I highly recommend laying out a daily schedule, but let's start simply with a morning routine that has both a workout in it, and without it. Plus, add an evening preparation bedtime routine component.

My morning routine looks like this on workout days:

Wake: 15 minutes of bathroom, dress with workout gear (already laid out), drink 8 oz warm lemon water, with Himalayan sea salt and 1 oz of apple cider vinegar. I mix a greens product with 24 oz of water.

I set my clock to work for 45 mins on the most important item and work at my desk/home office. Take a 10 bio and gratitude break—3 things I am grateful for (in my Oak Journal)

Back on another 30 min work session

10 min bio and transition break (protein shake)

30 min lift / 30 min cardio

20 min sauna, 10 min reading, 10 min meditate

5–5:15 a.m. Wake up, 15 min routine

5:15–6 Work session

6–6:10 Break/gratitude

6:10–6:40 Work session

6:40–6:50 Break and shake

6:50–7:50 Lift/cardio

7:50–8:10 Sauna (daily read/meditate)

Only 2-hour routine if no workout—get protein shake before sauna

Figure out a morning routine and a bedtime routine that works for you. This routine serves me in my world, but you must find what works for you. Your morning routine will suffer if you have a poor nighttime routine and a lack of prep for the next day.

Advanced Pain Exchange

If you need help understanding the best use of your time, prioritizing, and staying focused each day, get a coach who will train you to take a comprehensive approach and hold you accountable.

- An investment in coaching should yield a seven times return.
- Do what the coach asks you to do, even if it feels counterintuitive.

"If you are depressed, you are living in the past; if you are anxious, you are living in the future; if you are at peace, you are living in the present."

– Lao Tzu

8

Four Losing Behaviors and the Quadrant of Death

WE HAVE DISCUSSED many ways to build your winning team and strategies and techniques employed by athletes who transition these skills to leading business and organizations. But there is a killer inside your organization—four, in fact—and it is destroying the foundation of your team every day. You can stop it! You must be aware of these four killer behaviors that seem so innocent but prevail inside your organization already.

This is about gaining awareness to know how much your foundation is possibly eroding and how quickly the organization you built will crumble when your foundation can no longer hold the team and structure it's built on.

In this chapter, we will explore the behaviors that are working at destroying your team and organization from within: excuses, blame, quitting, and ignoring the data.

Excuses

You've heard about my affinity toward leaders who take responsibility and step up. Excuses are the opposite of saying, "I will." Excuses undermine the very thing that keeps your processes and productivity so high—accountability.

Each excuse brings more elasticity to the boundaries of accountability that have been established. It is a slow shift to a culture where "responsibility" is no longer valued and projected as one of the key attributes to being a successful team.

It's a bad look. Many people have been given a pass on these excuses; teachers, coaches, parents, and other authority figures in your life have allowed you to progress and "get away" with these behaviors, not fully knowing their lack of accountability in this area had hindered and hampered your growth, and made you a less desirable teammate for your current or future organization.

The largest hindrance to your growth is that awareness is never realized for you. Are the excuses due to a fear of failure, or your own reluctance to confront personal shortcomings or challenges? When one is not in an environment that will allow for mistakes and opportunities to gain experience and grow, deflecting responsibility feels like the route to take.

Unhealthy habits are formed here, and sometimes it is so subtle, a person may not even realize that this behavior is woven into the fabric of their interactions with others. People gently pull away from them, and it can become a desolate island for work and social interactions. It is not good, and then folks begin to rationalize with themselves. "I work better alone. Others just slow me down."

Encouraging open communication and acknowledging setbacks helps us improve and learn more efficient and better ways to do something.

Blame

Blame is another tactic from a person who is unwilling to take responsibility. It poisons team dynamics when not kept in check. There are three big losses from this losing behavior. First, trust is lost rapidly. When you have the blame game consistently on the horizon and used frequently, trust erodes until not a single person feels comfortable working with the team or person this behavior is associated with. Second, communication breaks down. Team members begin to "hold their cards close to their vest" and become conscious that an opinion or suggestion can be easy fodder for the next blame for a failure or miscommunication. The result is that vulnerability within the team is out of reach, and people share fewer ideas and provide less feedback. Everyone becomes more concerned with the backlash of the blame game over uniting for the greater good of accomplishing our initiatives. And third, collaboration goes out the window and becomes nearly impossible. Who wants to collaborate with people who use the blame game as a weapon? No one. Therefore, no one is looking to join that team.

Even when there is success, skillful players of high integrity want to be off the team. They know it's only a matter of time before a teammate "rolls over on them" and they become the target of the next blame. Collaboration is reduced with every thought and notion, rather than verbalized. This puts most of the team on high alert and on the defensive. What team works well under those conditions? None.

The finger-pointing game is a volatile one that has much more to do with the person doing the pointing than the one who is being pointed at. One person poisons the culture well, and not only is team morale going to take a hit, but individual well-being will be the next drop. No one wants to work for an organization where their personal well-being is jeopardized regularly. Good folks and outstanding team members have options. Why would you risk losing your best contributors?

First, stop the behavior. Have a one-on-one meeting. Reprimand privately and praise publicly. Let the person know that the blame-game is unbecoming and not tolerated. We foster teams that have shared responsibility for both successes and failures. This is one key element of the North Star of our vision to keep us aligned. Everyone must play their role and manage their responsibilities for us to achieve the outcomes for which we are striving. When we view mistakes collectively, the entire team can focus on determining not only the root cause of the issue but finding solutions to resolve the challenges—as opposed to assigning fault. As I'm looking to gather people on my teams who are both resilient and united, I'm looking for a mindset that values team and hyper-learning from errors and mistakes. Placing blame is a deterrent to all I hold dear to the best teams in the world.

Quitting

Quitting has profound consequences as individuals compromise their own potential, but bigger still is the creation of a void that impacts the entire team. Quitting shows up in several ways, but the most common is giving up on tasks, or simply disengaging from the team.

I find quitting to be one of the most contagious behaviors. On hard days, we may fantasize on our way home from work about doing something else that "we may be better suited for." It is not a real condition or true thought, but we entertain the feelings and thoughts when times are tough. It is a bit of human nature. When a teammate acts on something that may grossly resemble our fantasy, the first response is often relief for a quitter. They have limited, or restricted, their responsibilities and that feels incredibly good in the short term. But we are looking for team members who understand the discipline of short-term sacrifice for long-term benefit!

The other major challenge of quitting behavior is that it is a silent team killer. No one is in full understanding of why a team-mate has checked out or, worse, left the organization without expla-nation. Sometimes this seems like an easy road and a short-term solution to a much larger challenge. The fact is that quitting is rarely a sacrifice of discipline. It typically involves a yield to strong emotion, or fatigue. The negative ripple effect from quitters is substantial—and most never experience it because they are not part of the ripple effect.

The first time a quitter is subjected to an additional 15 work hours per week for 4 to 6 weeks to make up for a teammate who has left, they may finally come to understand their own behavior and its overarching reach on our teammates.

One of the major challenges is the silence of quitting. Without explanation, someone checks out, or is no longer willing to contribute, or give effort for the alignment of the team. The rest of the team will "backfill" the why in their own minds. It is only natural for humans to try to regulate what their teammate is thinking that caused all this pain. Some will look to the benefits for the person quitting, but words like selfish, inconsiderate, disrespectful, and others that are worse fill our minds. We don't even know the reason, and our minds turn dark as the ripple effect slams into our work and time. The mind has a tendency to manifest more on the negative side than the positive when unchecked. And quitting is usually without a lot of notice or explanation, so folks build up the reasons in their own mind.

Early detection of quitter behavior is crucial. One of the key elements of our Bloom Growth tools is a weekly meeting. Things get measured, and if quitting behavior shows up in the numbers and KPIs, then you're going to know quickly. Be determined to catch this behavior *early*! Build support for a team effort where everyone carries their engagement levels at a high standard. Assure that open dialogue and communication is always in season and available; provide support for those who are struggling with key areas of their responsibilities; be vigilant to see signs in major emotional swings, body language, and demeanor toward teammates and others; and watch closely for isolation from others and flippant attitudes. Address these behaviors promptly and do not let them fester and grow. This mentality is an internal plague that can affect people when left alone to "work itself out." Soon others could be infected with a quitter's mentality—a death plague to good teams. When meeting in person, reinforce the purpose of their role and the purpose of their contributions that the organization benefits from so they can understand their significance to the team and help reignite a team member's motivation.

Ignoring the Data

Teams are given numerous tools to collect data and help the team make informed decisions, and drive success. The subsequent behavior of ignoring the data will ultimately lead to increased risks and missed opportunities. The data, when collected objectively, reduces risks. Whether the behavior is driven by a lack of awareness for what should be measured, or reluctance to confront inconvenient truths, the neglect of data will undermine our team's ability to make informed choices and decisions.

"In God we trust; all others must bring data."

– W. Edwards Deming

The first time I heard the Deming quote I was immediately intrigued to recognize my own trust issues and my nature to be skeptical and scrutinize the logic of other people. I like to see data behind decisions leaving me to feel more informed and more positive about the decisions being made.

A team culture that instills a data-driven mindset is always welcomed. What does that look like? First, promote curiosity about our KPIs and the data you are measuring. Second, celebrate the decisions that you feel are strongly based on evidence rather than based on experts' assumptions. Finally, give your teammates the tools they need to compete on the digital and data front with modern technology and make the gathering of the data as efficient as possible. The power of great data equals greater solution-focused abilities and better-informed choices.

Decide which type of team you are going to have. Winners who find a way to win? Or teams that continue to get slowed by losing behaviors? I equate this to running the 400-meter race where one lane is on the inside of the track and is pristine and ready for racing, while the other lane is on the outermost lane and looks like the steeplechase, with a number of both high and low hurdles and maybe a pole vault pit thrown in for giggles. If the two runners are even close to equal in ability, they are not going to finish at the same time. The runner in the outside lane just went through an obstacle course, as opposed to the unimpeded inside lane. Do not let your lane be filled with any deterrent to your team, especially incurred within your own team, so that you get to where you want to go with the most efficiency possible.

Cultivate Winning Behaviors

Build recognition and commitment to addressing the four losing behaviors quickly and squash these behaviors before they get a foothold on your culture. Team leaders can shape the winning culture by modeling winning behaviors and limiting any losing ones, plus taking responsibility when or if they have a moment of weakness. Leaders should:

1. Foster accountability:
   - Have a daily huddle with your team.
   - Make weekly meetings fun and invigorating (ask me how).
   - Clarity on roles and responsibilities should be reviewed regularly.
   - Own your responsibilities; you are responsible for your results.

2. Encourage a blame-free environment:
   - Catch people encouraging and helping others.
   - Statements must not begin with "you" or "they."
   - If you're having an issue with a team member, take it to them in private first, one-on-one,

3. Prevent any quitting mentality from manifesting:
   - Be aware of words of "overwhelm," like "It's too hard" or "I'm struggling."
   - At the first sight of not getting work completed, come alongside to correct course and clarify expectations.
   - Manage a teammate by agreement, discussing work in increments and check-ins to monitor progress.

4. Embrace a data-driven mindset:
   - KPIs are clear.
   - Good solutions are enacted and backed up with KPIs and data.
   - Regular industry or internal metrics for meetings reinforce the value of data.

With strength from these big four winning behaviors, teams can build a foundation for long-term success and sustainability and navigate any challenges along the way.

Commit to the strategies above through ongoing communication, mentorship, and dedication to individual and team growth. Teams can transform destructive habits into constructive ones, ensuring that they not only survive the tough challenges, but excel through any adversity.

Jeremy Spann (or Spann, as we call him) is an intense person. I love him. We are cut from the same cloth. His superpower is he can discern information extremely quickly and at a depth most cannot comprehend. It leaves him five or more steps ahead of his competition, and sometimes his team members. While he is speaking to steps four and five of the challenge, his team members are still on one or two and he is whizzing past them. It is hard to keep up with someone who has an extremely rapid thought process.

All our superpowers are both blessings and curses. Recognize and be grateful for the blessing, but be aware of the negative impact or challenge it may bring. As Spann explained the Quadrant of Death, I could clearly hear in his voice the deeper implications of these behaviors rearing their head in a forward position from his military combat and police work. Though the implications are less likely to lead to life and death in our organizations, an ending of any kind is often considered a death of some type.

Have you seen these behaviors play out inside your own organizations and teams? The thing that struck me here is the heightened intensity of this matrix where the consequences intensify as an added element comes into play on our teams. The alarming reality of the mathematical equation in the quadrant is substantial.

Quadrant of Death

Jeremy Spann, CEO, STACKs Real Estate; Police Officer (retired); US Marine Corp

Spann (as his friends call him) is a good friend and fellow member of the Entrepreneurs' Organization. I first met Spann on a trip to Fort Worth when he graciously hosted a group of our high school hockey members at his shooting club.

I also was invited to join Spann's podcast, *Winning Strategies Playbook*, where we had fun talking shop for an hour on my background in coaching, his experiences with the military and law enforcement, and living in our crazy entrepreneurial worlds. I later welcomed Spann to *Winners Find a Way* for a special Veterans Day broadcast.

TRENT: TELL ME ABOUT THE KEY AREA OF DEVELOPMENT KNOWN AS THE QUADRANT OF DEATH.

Spann: The Quadrant of Death is ego, entitlement, blame, shame. And if you are operating on any one of those, that is *not good*. If you are operating in two of the four at any time, that is *bad*. If you are operating in three of the four, that is *dangerous*. And if you are operating in four of the four, it is *catastrophic*.

We have a saying in our company, like in the military: cease-fire. So if somebody witnesses an unsafe situation, they say, "Cease-fire! Cease-fire!" and everybody starts repeating, "cease-fire, cease-fire," and everybody stops, looks around, and then you adjust the situation.

And any team member can do it for me because I have found myself in the quadrant at times. And so, if you're in the quadrant, get out of the quadrant! Ego is the biggest one that I fall into. And it is number one because it's super easy to get there!

(continued)

(*continued*)

But the biggest one we see a lot of times is blame. "You're blaming, why are you blaming?" And they will say, "Well, that person did me wrong." And I say, "Okay, maybe they did. Are you going to live in this?" The response: "I'm angry blaming."

And so what you must do is have a very structured morning. And I'm not a structured person. I hate routines. I mean on Culture Index, I'm a low D. I am a nonconformist. I do not want to break any laws because I do not want to go to jail. But I want to break all the rules. I want to be a typical entrepreneur. I want to disrupt, but I have to be structured in my morning routine.

When Spann first spoke of this on my podcast, it immediately grabbed my attention. I wanted to unravel this web of ego, entitlement, blame, and shame. I have felt them all personally and have seen the harmful effects on teams.

Root of Discord

It all seems to start with ego, doesn't it? It is like the kiss of death, and it's often at the heart of the quadrant! A healthy ego transmits resilience and confidence, but the other side is an unchecked ego—a destructive force leading individuals to choose their own opinions over empathy, collaboration, and prioritize their own desires over others. It is a root of discord!

Ego is my number one challenge. If I could look at the worst five moments of my life, the errors all came from my ego, pride, and arrogance. Ouch! But if I look at each instance from 5,000 feet (a great lens to peer through), it's clear where it all takes a sharp downturn—my ego is bruised, or there is an inflated self-value. In each instance, had the ego been checked, the results could have been improved and likely the disastrous results averted.

Self-awareness is necessary in navigating this treacherous terrain for each of our team members.

The Poisoned Fruit of Privilege

Entitlement is often referred to as "the poisoned fruit of privilege." It emerges as the toxic byproduct of unchecked ego. If we have now added two of the four death quadrant behaviors, things are going to start to get bad.

When individuals believe they deserve special treatment or privileges without necessarily earning them, others who are actually earning them will immediately hold these folks in contempt. This sense of entitlement tends to permeate across both personal and professional settings. The downstroke effects it may have on individuals, teams, and society at large are staggering.

Avoidance Mechanism

Rearing its head again in this chapter (that is how prevalent it truly is), we return to the fact that this behavior is often a coping mechanism and has much more to do with the person "blaming" others.

I consider blame the opposite of taking responsibility. Adding this behavior on top of the first two (or any combination of) signifies a danger zone. Raise the red flag, or whatever you must do. All are at risk now, and no one is immune from the damage of the combined behaviors.

The issue of blame perpetuates a cycle of negativity and finger-pointing. We must consider the negative consequences of a blame-centric mindset on personal growth, relationships, and organizational dynamics. The psychology of outward blame versus inward condemnation are issues to dive into with teammates. The behavior is a sign of significant inner turmoil. Do not gloss over this behavior when it is presented consistently by teammates.

Silent Destroyer

I have read a great deal about the shame-driven cycle and a tough thing about this powerful behavior is that it is a silent force! The calm waters on the surface really do not pose a threat, but just below we are limited to whatever oxygen is in our lungs, and that is it. The shame inside is a silent killer, and we are not hearing the levels of danger that could be extremely elevated. Mental and emotional well-being are on high alert when shame is present. Shame has the potential to destroy self-esteem and hinder personal development, whether brought on internally or imposed by others.

Math Reality

We get to a point of no return when all four behaviors coexist. Most organizations don't have the resources to course correct and the damage levels and challenges mount when there is a mindset leading to a perfect storm of destruction. Outside help is often needed to salvage the organization with comprehensive intervention. The organization is now at a catastrophic level. Many do not survive if they have ignored the behaviors and decide they must confront it now or are still unwilling to make tough decisions. The organization is likely to have to make major changes through firings and removing the worst actors from the organization.

If you're struggling, assess the severity of your situation mathematically. Dissect and understand all the components. This is not a small feat for any leader as you look to balance human nature, awareness, and intentional efforts to foster positive behaviors. It will be essential to averting a potential catastrophic outcome that is lurking with the Quadrant of Death.

Key Takeaways

- Excuses avoid responsibility and hinder personal and professional growth.
- Blame damages team dynamics and collaboration.

- Quitting impedes resilience and perseverance.
- Ignoring the data restricts informed decision-making and improvement.
- Winning teams take ownership, focus on solutions, are resolute, and drive success on evidence-based decisions.

The Pain Exchange

All losing behavior must be stopped as soon as possible—nipped in the bud and stopped in their tracks. Fully know that these behaviors do not just "go away." They will rear their heads again and again. I'm not looking for a scorekeeping tab on who errs and slips back to these losing behaviors. I'm looking for a fun way to build awareness of the impact it is having on the team and how we can turn it into a positive.

Drop a Dime: Buy a large glass jar, and each time a person shows or speaks one of the losing behaviors, the team has permission to call it out with a "Drop a Dime" response. The person who is charged with the losing behavior must drop a dime in the glass jar! The physical and tactile act of stopping what they are doing, paying the nominal fine for the infraction, and then releasing that behavior to the jar as "paid for" is going to help limit and then eliminate these behaviors within teammates and us.

Each quarter or some other period, use the money in the jar to have a party, give the money to a charity, or creatively use these funds for something good and helpful for someone else, thus turning negative moments into a greater good.

9

The Big Leap: Setback to Stardom

Get a Rainout

The famous movie *Bull Durham* reiterates the fatigue of a long baseball season, and on a long road trip, Crash Davis (played by Kevin Costner) states, "I can get us a rain out!" His fellow players are worn out and just need the slightest reprieve and a day off during the dog days of August.

The reality is that professional athletes—and those who are the best in the world at anything—are preparing to perform daily with practices and performances. And they have been at this torrid pace since they were 10 to 13 years old! Their talent was undeniable and so they were thrust into the limelight playing for the top teams and competing (or performing) for the best organizations. And when not on the rigid and demanding schedules of games or performances, the training remains a grind, with heavy workloads for continuous improvement.

That is, until an injury or break in our cycles of performance hinders us from competing. A setback occurs, and then what? Most athletes have never had six months off from playing in the last decade or two. And that becomes a major challenge as a spectrum of emotions are happening and flooding the brain.

Stardom

Several players have returned from injury and rose far above their projected potential. The setback proved to be the catalyst to increase the players' urgency and focus and gave them time to assess all that they were doing in the programs previously to get marked improvements. This made them stronger and better across key areas, giving them fewer weaknesses and areas to exploit—and sometimes helping them discover hidden superpowers that had been underutilized when another strength was overexploited because it was the very thing that catapulted the player to their current level of success.

Orel Hershiser was a pitcher and the World Series MVP in 1988. Then in 1990 he had a major shoulder reconstruction through capsular shrinkage. He returned to pitch for another nine years afterward, earning 105 wins after the surgery, compared to the 99 prior. Orel was diligent in his work on his mechanics, physical health, and mental preparation, and was physically a much better athlete post-surgery than he was prior because of his efficient efforts.

Stephen Strasburg was rolling through the minor leagues and made his major league debut within two years, only to be injured at the end of his first season in the majors. Stephen's rehabilitation meant he was down for the first time in his life since he was eight. He went on to have a fantastic career throughout the 2010s, culminating in the World Series MVP in 2019.

Does the adage "You can't make the club in the tub" apply? Of course it does. But there are exceptions. The difference is that at the professional level, there are benefits to having a setback. The teams have hired the best in the world to look after their $250+ million inventory. Recruiting and signing players is an expensive deal. And most folks don't know that in addition to the 25-person active roster in the majors, there is a 40-person roster that includes protected prospects, as well as 200 or more minor league players who are playing in various leagues and training regularly out of the team's spring training facility. This is now almost a year-round proposition and offering for teams. Plus, most have a Dominican

Republic facility that contracts players for development at 16 years of age.

Playoff hero Francisco "Frankie" Rodriguez, affectionately known as K Rod, was a four-year overnight sensation at 20 years old in 2002 for the World Champion Los Angeles Angels. Frankie was signed at 16 years old with a lightning bolt for a right arm (95+ mph), and a body that rivaled the tallest eighth-grade player on the basketball team, and who weighed under 130 pounds. He did not look like that at his major league debut four years later!

Pro sports are a job of continuous improvement with a comprehensive approach to so much detail that there is not a single day when a coach will ever tell a player, "There is nothing left to work on." So when a setback occurs, for most players this is the first time they are forced to sit down for an extended period. Players may take a month or six weeks off, but training begins again after four weeks of rest, and skill training is critical to maintain during a heavier training off-season regimen of physical development. It is extremely important for players to maintain specific skill sets and fine motor skills while working diligently to make physical gains. Mental and moral training should accompany the severe off-season rigors.

There is nothing more motivating than to see your potential dreams threatened by injury, or worse, a setback that is out of your control. An athlete is never more "ready" and "coachable" than the time they face the final potential of being cut, dismissed, or retired due to injury.

Strict Training

It's common for athletes who are recuperating from an injury to have an identity crisis. While they likely will continue to participate in team meetings, strategy sessions, and developmental programs doing "what you are able to do given your limitations," they may describe themselves as the injured and maimed animal that is slowing the herd and unable to keep up.

It is time to go into strict training and look at every way to improve and prepare for a return to action. Players will review mechanics and sit with coaches for hours analyzing running gates, swing mechanics, arm angles, root causes of injury, training protocols not only to rehabilitate but pre-habilitate frequent areas of injury. Diets are disciplined and focused and the increased focus and energy of intent on every detail changes an athlete's mindset and work capacity.

The result is a major tune-up of an athlete who was considered to have the right tools to be a contributor to a team, and at the pinnacle of the sport, but now that athlete is improved in all aspects of the game—physically, mentally, morally, and emotionally. They have worked and prepared like at no other time in their careers, because when limited in some capacity, they ramp up on *all* areas that are available for improvement. Luckily for the athlete, most clubs will hire staff with this skill set to bring players along to the next level and beyond.

A person in recovery pivots into self-preservation quickly and men like me, who are experts at bringing people up to their peak level through an extremely comprehensive approach, dive into this new ball of clay. We shape every single edge and corner to create superhumans, and the hyper-learnings are off the chart. The athlete returns to play significantly better than before because all the other areas of focus and daily grind of the focused improvement have limited weaknesses and created superpowers!

Subconscious Reprogramming
Scott Fox, Former College Athlete; Mental Health and Sports Performance Practitioner; Author, *The Champions Playbook*

Scott has a passion for sports, having been a college athlete and now with a son competing in college sports. He also has a passion for athletes and their mental game.

Scott himself lives with chronic pain. Scott joined *Winners Find a Way* to discuss his work with subconscious reprogramming for athletes.

TRENT: A LOT HAS BEEN SAID ABOUT THE MIND AND WORKING BACK FROM A SETBACK. WHERE DOES YOUR FOCUS LIE?

Scott: I do not do sports psychology; what I do is subconscious reprogramming. And I do it through the body and the mind. We are athletes, and from a holistic perspective you can access spirit through the body; it's all connected. And so for us to say, "Hey, the solution for mental health or the solution for sport performance is only through the mind," that is not correct. At least it's not full. And I want to have something that is full.

WHEN THINGS GET HARD AND SETBACKS HAPPEN, HOW IMPORTANT IS IT THAT PEOPLE ARE MINDFUL OF THEIR PURPOSE?

"Winning in life is to acknowledge what your calling is. What is your heart saying? Not your head, because your head is going to reflect society. What is your heart's calling? What is that imprinted divine message that's on your heart, and then do you live in accordance with that?"

– Scott Fox

Athletes are assessed in so many ways during a setback, and perseverance is critical. Confidence is lost and must be found. All the prep, but low on the reps. Self-awareness is developed at a higher level. An athlete must be resolute in staying on the course and keeping the focus on what they are pursuing and how the thing they're most enthusiastic about is on purpose.

The time to face the music and the test of your character is when you have a setback. When athletes get injured and their current stats are 195 pounds with 15% body fat, then return to a team four months later at 215 pounds and 10% body fat, the changes are palpable. Everyone is watching to see how they utilized their time while down. Did they get better? How did they respond to maximize the future outcome? All the staff are watching.

Overcomers

Justin Breen, Master of Abundance and Visionary; Author and Mindset Champion; Journalist; Entrepreneur

Justin is a hard charger who lives life to the max! Justin continually works with top performers and is a Kolbe and Strength Finders Assessment advocate, as well as a strategic coach proponent. Continuous improvement is always on the menu with Justin. He has been on *Winners Find a Way* twice.

TRENT: WE GOT DEEP INTO A FEW THINGS THE FIRST TIME YOU WERE ON THE PODCAST, AND I WANTED TO BRING YOU BACK TO EXPAND ON THE COMMON DENOMINATORS YOU'VE SEEN IN TOP ACHIEVERS.

Justin: I have not met one top performer at the highest level—I am not talking about regular humans, I'm talking about people at the highest level—who have not overcome at least one of the following four things, and most overcome two or three, to become successful. This is what separates the one-percenter, like me, from everyone else:

- Bankruptcy or potential bankruptcy
- Depression
- Anxiety
- Traumatic experiences as a child or young adult

Most people use those as excuses their entire life, but top leaders at the highest level figure it out and are grateful.

> *"When you are constantly grateful you can't be ungrateful. My entire life is good habits and good patterns. You cannot have bad habits and bad patterns and get good results. It's pretty simple."*
>
> *– Justin Breen*

No Victims Here

As Justin Breen states, there is no time to stay down, so get back up. You have been dealt a blow, but you move through it. Any movement into victimhood and "woe is me" attitude will limit your solution strategy and steal your freedom. You take action and though you do not have to love the situation, you do have to accept the current reality and recognize that you need a new future reality. Once a person gets very clear with the utmost specificity about where they see themselves in that future reality and have written out a full description of what that reality will look like with detailed measurements and KPIs to support the vision, it becomes relatively easy to design the workload and performance requirements to take a top player from the current reality to the future reality. You should have specific timelines to plan the workload and make it both comprehensive and strategic. There will be no wasted efforts and all efficiencies will be counted. The plan is simple and forthright. The execution is not easy but the margin for error and inefficiency is nearly nonexistent.

Gaining Freedom
Michael Levin, Author and Publisher; Attorney

Michael is a best-selling author and publisher, a two-time *New York Times* and three-time Amazon nonfiction best-seller. He is busy in the world of books with ghostwriting, production,

(continued)

(continued)

and teaching writing to others. Business leader Jay Abraham referred to him as the Master of the Business Fable.

Michael is a fellow baseball enthusiast and sings with the Tanglewood Festival Chorus of the Boston Symphony Orchestra. He is also sober for more than 29 years.

We had a lot of subjects to cover as Michael joined me on *Winners Find a Way*.

TRENT: WE SEE TEAMS STRUGGLING WITH FOLKS WHO ARE LOST AND LIKELY NOT IN THE RIGHT SEAT FOR THEIR TEAM. WHAT WOULD YOUR ADVICE BE TO SOMEONE WHO THINKS THIS IS NOT WHAT THEY ARE MEANT TO DO?

Michael: Quit complaining. I always say that if you don't like your job, the reality is that you have somebody else's job, and you just don't like their job. Then where is *your* job? Where is the thing that you're meant to do? Where is the business that you're meant to create? Create wealth and create jobs and create opportunity and create great results for people. Go do that!

HOW WOULD YOU RECOMMEND PEOPLE GET OVER THAT TIPPING POINT FROM BEING GREAT TO BEING OUTSTANDING?

You do a good job. But you only get rewarded if you do a great job at something, and you get good results. Why? Because a lot of people are great at what they do. And if you're outstanding, you get *all* the results. And the difference between being *outstanding* and being *great* is a smaller amount of work than most people think.

If you stay with it, all you'll need to do is to put out one more unit of effort, and you'll get 10 units of results.

YOU WERE AN ALCOHOLIC WHO LOST YOUR MATERIAL POSSES-
SIONS, BUT YOU KEPT THE KEY RELATIONSHIPS. WHAT WOULD
YOU TELL SOMEONE FACING A MAJOR CHALLENGE AND SETBACK
IN THEIR LIFE TODAY?

There is no shame in having a problem. The shame is having
a problem and not taking advantage of the help that is out
there. That's the real shame in life. It's no shame to be knocked
down to the ground; that's life. The real shame is to just lie
there. Nobody is giving you a 10 count. Nobody's waiting.
They're not gonna count you out at 10.

WHAT LIFTED THE VEIL ON YOUR ALCOHOLIC LIFESTYLE AND
BEHAVIOR AND HAS HELPED YOU STAY SOBER
FOR OVER 29 YEARS?

"When I was able to say, 'I am the problem, not them, not
her, not him, not the organization, not the incident.' When I
said, 'I'm the problem.' Now all of a sudden, I have freedom
to become the solution. I have the freedom to make changes."
– Michael Levin

COO Responsibility

The chief operating officer is responsible for the operations of an
organization. As the challenges come and the plans are strategized,
execution must take place. Be the COO of your life! Everything is
intentional and to address all the needs at this moment, the days
will be filled with little down time, and even that is scheduled and
planned—it's called recovery and regeneration. You've done everything planned for the day, achieved the day's goals. Then go to your
bed, prep for sleep for 30 minutes: review the next day's schedule,

relax, and read, and journal the day's successes and challenges. Then at 10 p.m. lights out—you should be exhausted! Sleep is your body's charger. Get it back to 100%. There is no one-and-a-half-hour supercharger for the body. It takes a full seven hours, at least.

Be responsible and accept your failures, errors, and mishaps. It's good to prove you're human like the rest of us. But by accepting your role in it all, you gain the freedom to make the changes that will help you find the solution—get a mentor, call someone who has done what you're doing, be a voracious reader, watch instructional videos, find the people who can help you and ask them for the help—then do it! Winners find a way to win! You have the freedom to change, so do it!

Mental Gymnastics for Balance

Todd Martin, Head of Tennis at Beemok Capital; CEO, International Tennis Hall of Fame; #4 ATP Ranked Tennis Player (retired)

Todd and I grew up in Michigan an hour from each other. People knew him as one of the best tennis players in the state. I was known as the best player for the four counties that surrounded me. Enormous difference.

Todd is a cerebral leader and tennis player. He is physically imposing at six-foot-four and plays exceptionally well on grass courts. His playing highlights include a Davis Cup Championship in 1995 for the USA over Russia. And he played in two Grand Slam finals, losing to Pete Sampras in Australia in 1994, and an epic battle with Andre Agassi at the 1999 US Open, where he lost in a five-set thriller after being up two sets to one.

Todd transitioned to leadership even while playing, getting involved in the Players Association, serving on the board of the USTA, then taking the role of CEO of the International Tennis Hall of Fame in Newport, Rhode Island.

TRENT: HOW DOES AN ATHLETE'S EFFORT REMAIN CONSISTENT ON A TOUR OF PLAYERS WHO ARE THE BEST IN THE WORLD?

Todd: On focused effort, I didn't win but I put myself in a position to win and it was because I accepted the fact that I did not have control over anything other than how hard I tried.

WHAT IS ONE THING YOU LEARNED FROM STARTING NEW THINGS AND VENTURING OUT OF YOUR COMFORT ZONE?

"Once you start, you're 50% done and that doesn't always work out to be exactly right, but the anxiety of doing something different or a large project that's in front of you is really and truly where the anxiety becomes the biggest hurdle that you have to clear."

– Todd Martin

WHAT IS YOUR ADVICE FOR SOMEONE FACING ADVERSITY AND NEEDING TO OVERCOME SOMETHING IN THEIR LIFE RIGHT NOW?

When you are down, time is your friend and enemy. Get busy taking action. Drive yourself to new effort levels and learning. Time seems to slow because your evenings, when performing, are filled with travel, games, fellowship, and competition. And when you're down, the evenings are quiet, and you have time to think about it all. This is part of the mental test and training. When you speak to yourself, speak well. The mental acuity gained during this time will be shaped and maturity will be attained. The benefits of this process will continue to make you better. Be mindful, present, and good to yourself.

Drawing Clarity from Tragedy

Kevin Santiago, Collegiate and Pro Baseball Hitting Instructor; Faithful Friend; Felon

Kevin and I were introduced at a men's ministry event. We had similar histories of both playing and coaching baseball. But Kevin's playing career ended earlier than mine, and he became a union member and shot up to leadership quickly.

Kevin had a few issues with work, and then he had a major personal life crisis with a relationship that ended poorly, and he was in a bad place spiritually, physically, emotionally, and mentally. He had even contemplated taking his own life.

One weekend, on a chilly day in early December in Chicago, Kevin met his friends to watch some football. He drank too much and drove under the influence. He went through a red light and hit a car, killing the driver.

His journey to prison and repentance is formidable, a hopeful story from a tragic event. It takes courage for someone to come on a public show and discuss their trespasses and mistakes in life. Kevin shows honor in doing it when he joined me on *Winners Find a Way.*

TRENT: AFTER A TRAGIC ERROR IN JUDGMENT AND ACTING OUT OF CHARACTER WHAT YOU KNEW YOUR HEART TO BE, WHY WAS SUPPORT THE KEY TO GETTING YOU BACK ON TRACK?

Kevin: I think when you're talking about support, that support is the good that comes out of it. And the people willing to put their name on the line and say, "Hey, I will sign up for this guy." As a young person or adult, anytime in your life that someone puts their name on the line for you, it is a big deal. We should not take that lightly.

After being convicted for the accident, what was the thing you learned most about yourself?

Before, I thought I knew right and wrong. But after a year and a half of training, of prepping my armor for prison (the armor of God, Ephesians 6:10–18); for what was about to happen and what's next, that line and that clarity is what I heard. After the training you have clarity now. I think a lot of us have a blurred line of right and wrong.

What have you learned about what's important for you on the journey?

I've had the money, the house, the car. It's not that I don't want it anymore, that would be great! But touching peoples' hearts, being here on the field, I tell everybody I get to go to work today. That is what is important to me.

What led you to seek the counsel and help you needed?

"When sentenced and headed to prison, there is guilt, shame and there are all sorts of things going on. I had to assess, 'So where are you at right now from a mental health standpoint?' PTSD, the anxiety, and the questions I had never dealt with before. I had no tools in the toolbox other than alcohol, which is not a tool, it is an enabler."

– Kevin Santiago

Get your heart and mind right, and your body will follow. Do not underestimate your power. Kevin took responsibility for his actions. He served his time, repented his ways, and is not going to return to prison ever. Though so many lives were negatively affected that night, he pushed forward with the purpose of living differently and being a light.

Your GPS

The GPS here is your own—your *growth positioning system*. Many of the best, when competing at the top, often feel like they are lucky because they were in the right place at the right time. I don't really believe in that. I believe that you must position yourself for the next opportunity. Being the best that you can be, right where you're at, proves to yourself and others that you can manage the responsibilities you have been given. When you exceed the expectations by going the extra mile, you are in position to receive the next opportunity.

You must be diligent and focused to maximize your **INTENT**:

I—**Imagine** your future reality with full clarity.

N—**Need goals** for your day, week, month, and quarter.

T—**Target reason** for exactly why this matters so much.

E—**Extensive plan** for the how you will execute on getting yourself in position (it's okay not to know at first and to ask for help from someone who has done what you are looking to accomplish).

N—**Necessary execution** is vital. No inefficiencies and distractions.

T—**Trusted advisor** is an accountability partner who is vested in your success.

Key Takeaways

- Injuries allow for reset and focus on strict training, mechanics, fitness, sleep, and specific areas of weakness.
- Mental awareness, drive, and aligning with purpose supports peak performance.
- The best in the world overcome serious challenges and use the learnings from them to succeed.

- Complaining and victimhood is the sickness, and taking action is the cure.
- Take responsibility for the past, present, and future.
- Be the COO of your personal development plan to position yourself for future opportunities.
- Leave your comfort zone with support and guidance for intentional preparation.

The Pain Exchange

Take a long weekend, or three-day goal planning retreat. Grab your journal and spend the first two days writing out exactly how you want things to look in 12 months. Be descriptive and write in detail about eight categories:

1. Physical health: exercise/fitness; nutrition; sleep

2. Mental and emotional well-being: self-awareness/EQ; stress management; clarity/focus

3. Moral conditioning: daily reading; journaling; small group; fellowship; values

4. Intellectual growth: continuous learning; Continuing Education Units; critical thinking; problem-solving; expanded knowledge

5. Career/professional development: work goals; upskill/expertise; prioritization; efficiency

6. Financial mastery: spending plan; saving/investment plans; large purchase planning; asset management

7. Interpersonal relationships: effective communication; healthy relations; conflict resolution; empathy

8. Charity and contribution to others: community support; global reach; volunteer; mentor; give back

Here are some other categories to consider: family/team health; people; data management; strategy/process plan; technology management; purpose statement; vacation/recreation/travel.

Advanced Pain Exchange

Day 3: Use the link to grab your one-pager Bloom Growth™ plan and give clarity to your vision. Visit https://1drv.ms/b/s! AtQ-sVKRFiozhO1eGUM-i71GdPmV5Q?e=HGbTN0 and use the password "LeadingWinningTeams" (expires: 12/31/25).

10

Coaching, Communication, and Clarity, Oh My!

Sports have always reflected life. Our culture has currently lost its way on this. The stories of triumph and loss are equally gripping. The stakes are higher than ever. The levels of pressure to win and for fame are now at a level of the professional ranks, but for 14-year-olds! The challenges of trained athletes at peak levels are immense. Each athlete at that level has trained and prepared well for tens of thousands of hours that would yield an expertise belonging to the few who compete with the best. But as parents, we have fallen into this trap of the kids getting this level of knowledge and understanding in a noticeably brief time at incredibly young ages.

Character Developer

Parents are paying a great deal of money to club programs, and "experts," to gain an advantage to outperform their fellow competition. Unrealistic expectations mean kids are running away from sports earlier, and maybe some they genuinely enjoy, because it is no longer enjoyable.

We got lost at the massive exchange of dollars for values. We have forgotten that youth sports are truly about the character development of a young person and the life lessons that can be experienced through sports. We are measuring the wrong things. The key performance indicators are not Wins and Losses, Trophies, or All-Star Game Selections!

The Human Condition

Tim Mead, President, National Baseball Hall of Fame and Museum (retired); Los Angeles Angels Front Office Executive

Tim has been a friend since 1999 when I signed with the LA Angels. He is known as the nicest guy in baseball and for being the glue of the organization to make sure we all stick together and stay aligned.

Tim has worn many hats in professional baseball, and ultimately became president of the National Baseball Hall of Fame in Cooperstown, New York. He retired from baseball and from the HOF and is enjoying his grandkids and family in Southern California.

Speaking on some of the deeper issues of professional sports teams is always interesting. As with all companies, there are plenty of challenges. The interview was just what I had hoped for.

TRENT: WHEN TOUGH DECISIONS NEED TO BE MADE, HOW DO YOU BOIL IT DOWN TO GETTING IT RIGHT?

Tim: What it boils down to is your own inner thoughts. You can ask so many people: What should I do? What do you think? And at the end of the day, I believe it's what your heart tells you to do and mine was pick yourself up and go play baseball.

IS FEEDBACK A GIFT?

Personally, I want constructive criticism. I just said this recently to somebody about me. "Nobody can be harder on me when something goes wrong then me."

LEADERS MUST MAKE TOUGH DECISIONS ABOUT PEOPLE. WHAT HAVE YOU LEARNED FROM HIRING AND FIRING OVER THE YEARS?

Several years ago, I probably waited too long for a team member and none of us wanted to fire someone. None of us want to let go of folks because it will affect a lot of people. When we do not make the right decision in that regard, we are not respecting ourselves for eventually affecting our own families and we're not instructing that person who needs a shake-up, to better their careers for the future.

And by that, I don't believe you ever fire somebody unless they've done something terribly wrong. You should have had a conversation with them and come alongside to help them. Nobody should be blindsided. I think when we see that with the underperformers, we see that there's a lack of system in place of communication to review and track.

WHAT IS YOUR DAILY PHILOSOPHY OF GETTING THE WORK DONE AND BEING YOUR BEST?

"I'm a firm believer that every day I go to work I want to get better at my shortcomings rather than half of my strengths. So, I think the advice is just very simple: None of us have it all licked; we know inside even the most."

– Tim Mead

The Gift

Feedback is a gift. I want it all the time, even though sometimes I do not enjoy it at the moment. I surround myself with winners. And winners find a way to win. They are resourceful, respectful, adaptive, and experienced. When I have seen my friends, employees, mentors, coaches, and peers be successful at so many levels, I want to learn more about them and about me.

The feedback from people who have been through trials, like athletes, comes from a world of experience and knowledge. Their feedback will be based on their own experiences and learnings, not necessarily on your condition. A shared experience comes from the heart of one person to another. What happened: the effect of that challenge, the outcome, and then the magic—the learning. The learning is often incongruent with the outcome. Weird, right?

Not at all, really.

The challenge I see every day is folks who refuse feedback, and the chance for hyper-learning. Knowledge is gained from a trusted advisor who is willing to come alongside and help you by sharing their wisdom and experience gained through the trials of their life. What a blessing and what a gift for someone to give. If you choose not to receive it, that's on you.

Coach and Teacher

My father was a teacher and a coach. His job was as a professor of accounting at a community college. He had a dry and witty sense of humor, and likely brought different perspectives to his teaching that most people in a business college did not bring. I learned later from his students that many lessons centered on the fodder and challenges of his four children, and the economics of raising them.

My dad was my coach for floor hockey, football, baseball, and more. If he understood the sport, he would be willing to come alongside and mentor me and my friends. It was a wonderful experience for me, as he was trained to teach.

I admired my dad as a person who studied the game and passed along wisdom to young kids playing the game. He was not the most brilliant coach but he brought tactics that would allow us to achieve and overcome. He was a teacher who had a superpower of breaking down the critical fundamentals of being successful in each sport, and then training us in the fundamentals of the sport until we understood and could perform those well.

Once a team has a commitment and clarity around the fundamentals and begins to achieve those at a much higher level than
their competition, winning becomes common. It was exclusive and
it was not because we had so much more talent. We were trained
and prepared and other teams were not.

My father taught us about caring for one another, having fun,
building our character of right and wrong, and being young boys
where our word meant something. If you said you would do it, you
should get it done.

We won a lot more than we lost, but the process was a fun
journey. We all wanted to win. I was one of those kids who was playing for the Stanley Cup, Lombardi Trophy, and World Series Ring
from the time I was 12—it was important to me. The perspective
that my father had was crucial to keep me from getting horribly out
of balance, as he certainly understood it was a 12U game, and the
major sports networks would not be covering this all-important
game out at Bailey Park at 5 p.m. on a Tuesday between Russell
Plumbing and Post 66! I was gaga to compete, and he knew it.

In the highly acclaimed show *Ted Lasso*, Ted understood that
"sometimes you win, but you lose. And sometimes you lose, but you
win!" Having a key leader with perspective changes the game for
kids and this is *not* an easy transition for me as a pro guy who has
studied all things sports, right down to the nitty-gritty of how to
maximize potential.

There's a phrase I use often with the parents of my 12-year-old
son's teams. The parents will voice frustrations over the gap of what
they see from their local minor league team or their favorite major
sports team, and unjustly compare their 12U kids' teams' performance to what they see on ESPN. I know how batty that sounds.
We laugh a little to lighten the experience and intensity, which gets
too high. I ground them with this simple line: "I know, sometimes
they act like they're 12 out there." The reaction to that is sometimes a double take, but it typically lands with a parent who catches
the reality that the comparison is unjust and incongruent to make.

It's fun when superb talent comes along and can outperform wonderfully even against kids who are older and have years more of experience. But we seem to forget the boy or girl is just an early teen, doing early teens things, like riding their bike, hanging out with friends, and studying. No need to rush these kids to a pro level, to put them in adult situations for which they are unprepared physically, mentally, emotionally, and often morally. High school is a time we reinforce and shape our children's moral compass. It is when they will develop the independence to evaluate all these learnings they have had from home, the classroom, church, and certainly from all their coaches. The legacy of sports is to train them up. For me, coaching has always been synonymous with teaching.

Culture of Communication

Ray Anderson, Athletic Director, Arizona State University; NFL Player Agent (retired); Harvard Law Graduate

Ray has been a champion of athletics and athletes for an extraordinarily long time. He has been the AD at ASU, coming from an NFL agency firm.

Ray's interview was one I looked forward to because his reputation preceded him, and he has had so many unique experiences throughout his life.

TRENT: WHAT'S THE MOST IMPORTANT THING FOR LEADERS TO GET THEIR ORGANIZATIONS MOVING IN THE RIGHT DIRECTION?

Ray: It's all for me about communication and having a cultural environment where everyone understands that they have a voice and we expect that they will use their voice without intimidation, without hesitation, without reserve.

YOU KEEP A CLOSE EYE ON THE CULTURE. HOW DO YOU MANAGE IT?

One of the things I tried to do whenever I could, and sometimes it would freak people out, is I would talk to the equipment manager. I'd want to talk to the ball boy to say, "Man, how's Lee really, as a guy? Is he cool? Is he respectful? Does he act like he's entitled to more than anybody else?" They will tell you a lot about a guy's character.

If you really want to judge the quality or the strength of the leader, just look at their staff. Pretty much tells you all you need to know because if your staff is strong, ethical, committed, and passionate, it means that you as a leader have done something right.

WHAT DO YOU WANT FROM YOUR LEADERSHIP TEAM?

If you are in a partnership and everybody agrees, then you need to get rid of everybody else because you don't need them. You want people who push back. If everybody agrees then you know you're duplicating effort because if everybody agrees, then you're not getting any better.

"You're only as good as the last guy on the roster. No one is beyond the work and dedication that it's going to take to be successful as a team."

– Ray Anderson

Review the Tapes

Video reviews have become amazing over the last 20 years, with really impressive technology. Shout-out to LiveBarn, an interactive camera in ice rinks that have continued to provide high-quality HD visibility in local rinks. Coupled with software like HUDL, it will track all sorts of KPIs of the ice hockey game—shots on goal, faceoffs won, score, and so on.

I have been challenged at the lower levels of hockey because introducing these tools at an earlier age is a game-changer for programs that are willing to use technology and data to create learning opportunities. Athletes at the highest levels are trained in all things numbers when it comes to statistics. Athletes are good at math. I think I enjoyed math as a kid because as a younger player I was so focused on batting average and on-base percentage. One negative was that I was starting to factor my average in the on-deck circle prior to an at-bat, likely to the detriment of being fully focused on the task at hand—hitting the ball and getting on base safely.

I'm utterly amazed at how few corporate teams are incorporating a significant strategy around "reviewing the tapes." Bring data! Once the data is collected, we can strategize what the data is telling us as a team.

Sales teams should be utilizing the results and learnings from each other and every opportunity. Small companies now compete easily with larger corporations because the tools have become increasingly affordable to grab and pinpoint data. Plus, small companies are more adaptable to innovative technologies with fewer users and thus quicker rollout and less training cost. The review on technology can be a game-changer for a small brand and put them on the map very quickly.

Open Lines

Despite early promises that innovative technology would bring communication to new levels, there is now less communication than ever, and clarity is at an all-time low. Instead, we all stare down the barrel (or screen) of information overload and are challenged to prioritize the information with which we are bombarded. Relationships have become secondary. We are not really "relating." Keeping the lines of communication open and having rules of engagement are critical. Athletes learn early that there is a chain of command and chain of communication to adhere to in any given organization, and it's not always the same. But it's critical to have clarity around how we discuss information, and how that information is moved between people and reported to team members. If there's conflict, team members must know the proper way to address one another and resolve matters in a cohesive and expeditious way.

Building the trust to create the space for the open lines of communication is not easy, but when done properly, people feel heard, like they matter, and know they have value so that the organization will give them the room to speak up.

Search for Truth

As we look to create a cohesive team, conflict will be a party to it. I like management expert Patrick Lencioni's take on the matter: "If we trust one another, healthy conflict is nothing more than a search for the truth."

If there were no conflict in the workplace, then machine learning would replace us very rapidly. But the human emotion side is important to a disagreement. We will dive deeper into this in Chapter 12.

Soler Listening

SOLER is a concept brought to me by the Entrepreneurs' Organization in my training on mentorship. Here is what the acronym means:

- **S—Sit:** Why would one person sit and the other stand? That creates an imbalance or power dynamic, as if one were "over the other." Sit to get level.
- **O—Open:** Be ready to listen, and that means shoulders up, no arm crossing, and ready to be open and present in all ways.
- **L—Lean in:** As if you're watching a great movie, be on the edge of your seat! Ready to learn and sponge it all up.

E—Eye contact: If you are a note taker, that's okay. Jot something down then look up and lock your eyes again to assure that you are fully invested, and the speaker knows you are listening.

R—Relax: In a one-on-one conversation, the speaker will often mirror, or reflect, the demeanor of the listener or interviewer. If you are calm and relaxed, so will your interviewee or a fellow teammate be. Establishing a safe space allows for people to open up and address key items in an environment of protection.

Key Takeaways

- Prioritize character development over winning in youth sports.
- Personal growth comes from constructive criticism and inner reflection.
- Feedback is a valuable learning tool, derived from experience.
- Effective coaching focuses on fundamentals and character.
- Open communication is crucial for strong leadership.
- Despite technology, communication has decreased, affecting clarity.
- Apply data analysis (like sports teams do) to corporate teams for improvement.
- Establish best practices for communication.
- Healthy conflict is a search for truth, and attitudes matter.

The Pain Exchange

Listeners are leaders. For this exercise you'll be working with your significant other, or someone else with whom you are in a close relationship, such as a family member. This is going to be a listening session, but do not tell them. Before beginning, decide what subject you're going to talk about. I typically ask, "What is the biggest challenge you're facing right now?"

- Choose a quiet spot with comfortable chairs in an area where you will not be distracted or interrupted. It should be away from other people so that confidentiality can be preserved—you don't want others hearing your discussion. Pour a cup of coffee or tea. Be in close proximity and use the SOLER techniques: sit, be open, lean in, make eye contact, and be relaxed.
- As a leader and listener in this conversation with this special person, sit together for a minimum of 10 minutes (but 15 minutes or more is encouraged) to practice listening, *not to offer advice*. I want you to listen for three things on a chosen subject matter:

1. The information/experience

2. How it makes them feel

3. How they behaved through the experience

You are only allowed to start any speaking with one of three phrases:

1. *Tell me more about* … *the biggest challenge you're facing today.* Examples: *What is going on [at work, with our daughter's teacher, with your lousy boss, the current challenge you're facing, in your world]?*

   You are listening for voice inflections and watching for shifts in their body language. You are watching for a shift in importance and meaning, and when you ask them to tell you more about it because their body language indicates that there's more to the story, they will drive deeper.

2. *What I heard you say was* . . . Reflect after a few minutes to assure the speaker that the whole story is being heard correctly. I do this often when speaking with technical team members from IT, or where there may be a language barrier.

I use this to slow down the chat and assure myself I'm tracking through certain technical points that are above my educational experience. I'm also doing this every five minutes to assure the person speaking knows I'm fully engaged. It challenges my listening and recall, and it makes the listener feel heard.

3. *And what else . . . ?* This is probably the most miraculous question I have ever used; I call it the great AWE question. The moment I say "and," it seems to trigger that person to look for more to say on the matter, or something related to it. I have used this with peers, direct reports, my customers, competitors (oh, they will talk—catch them at the bar on your next industry trade show and buy them a drink; it's magic!), and more.

I love to hear responses to this exercise! Please reach out to me on social media or at trent@leadershipity.com with the subject line AWE. The testimonials of deep listening for someone you genuinely care about can move your relationship to a new level. And you will *know* and understand the value of being an appreciated listener by their reaction, and feedback!

CAUTION: This is a *listening* exercise, not a *fixing the challenge* exercise. Despite your belief that you have brilliant advice and solutions for this person, suppress the desire to give that feedback on this occasion. This may be more difficult for some than for others.

11

Perseverance and Positioning

As WE EXPLORE the paths of the most successful people in sports, and as I speak to them about their journey, most do *not* talk about how important it was to be prepared when the opportunity came.

Positioned for Greatness

I tell a great many people that becoming the best is about positioning yourself for the opportunity by having a plan, getting a coach or accountability partner, putting in the work, and balancing all of it with clarity and intention.

Thousands upon thousands of athletes, and even more leaders, have faced challenges. Leaders have built formulas for success. Hit up your local bookstore, and you'll find all sorts of books on the subject, plus now we can find tutorials right on YouTube on how to do almost anything. The lessons are many and they are everywhere.

I have a confession. I know exactly what it takes to attain and sustain peak performance at the top levels in both sports and business. The reality is that most people will not do the work. And some do not have the God-given talent to compete at the top levels. But when parents come to me about their child becoming a pro athlete, and I start telling them what it takes, people realize it is a *lot* of work and there is no room for inefficiency. Every misstep and error can be a setback and a wasted day. The discipline it takes to compete at the top level is understated.

When going through every step of the journey, opportunities will come to those who have positioned themselves for the next level, those who ooze preparedness and mastery at their current level. Proving you can compete every time against the current competition is important. The folks who are looking at your skill set and evaluating you are seeing your potential and what you may be capable of. The challenge is that most folks are not fully locked into being the best at their current position and getting just a little bit better every day. Evaluators are not looking for people who give you three good days and then take a week off from their focus and performance. Consistency and continuous improvement are the name of this game.

You may only get one chance at the next level. The GM came to see you and they liked what they saw in game one, and tomorrow will be the true test. When you do not show up prepared and have a deficient performance, you may be set back two years until the next opportunity—if you can hang in that long. The coach may chime in with "It happens from time to time with this player. He's a bit inconsistent and has some maturing to do."

This is exactly what can and does happen. But don't you believe you owe it to the people who invested in you to give it your absolute best every day? All the people who sacrificed for you to get to where you are: your parents driving you to all these games and feeding you practice reps, a coach who mentors you, and many more. (Read and review more on the *growth positioning system*—GPS—in Chapter 9.)

Be Epic
Bryan Gillette, Ultra Marathoner; World Traveler; Author, *Epic Performance*

Bryan was introduced to me through a mutual friend. Runners have some of the highest discipline levels, and Bryan is an ultra guy. These races are not for the faint of heart.

His appearance on *Winners Find a Way* is a must listen. But here I want to extract from his book and focus on Bryan's mantra, EPIC.

ENVISION: VISUALIZATION FOR AND ON SUCCESS

You can't go towards the future unless you can see it. So the E is how you envision the big things.

PLAN: PUT A PLAN IN PLACE

Once you see what the future is like, how do you go ahead and put that plan in place? And one of the first things about the P in that plan is just start doing something.

ITERATE: WORK YOUR WAY UP AND THROUGH IT

I am iterating to the plan; you do not start playing in the World Series. You start in T-ball. And then you move to Little League, and you work your way up. You don't start running by entering a marathon. You start running two miles and it hurts. And then you run three miles, and it hurts. And you keep doing that and you work your way up. You don't start as the CEO of a company. You start off at a lower level and you work, you get success, and you build confidence. Confidence comes from successes at smaller levels. Be a "wayfinder."

COLLABORATE: LEARN FROM OTHERS, MENTORS, COLLEAGUES, AND MORE

C is collaborate—learn from somebody else. There really isn't anything new, and not a lot of new stuff out there that somebody hasn't done before. So learn from their successes, learn from their failures! And people are very willing to share, sow the seeds, and collaborate.

(continued)

(continued)

And lastly, you have to go out and perform it. So if you think about it like an ultra-marathoner, the EPIC concepts get you to the starting line; envision the plan, iterate, collaborate, and collaborate more, iterate again. The performance gets you from the starting line to the finish line. That's where you have to persevere. That's where the hard kind of stuff comes in.

"You can't go towards the future unless you can see it."
– Bryan Gillette

The Line of Decline
Chase Minnifield, NFL player; ACL and Achilles Rehabilitation; CEO, EZOS

Chase played in the NFL and is the son of a longtime NFL player, so he has the legacy thing, and I am sure that comes with lots of pressures and expectations. When I had Chase on *Winners Find a Way*, we talked about the difficulty of being ready and never wavering about when the call might come. He talked about the grind and how challenging it is to always be ready when, week after week, your number is not called.

TRENT: AS I LIKE TO SAY, "WE DO NOT GO RUNNING AWAY FROM WHAT WE KNOW IS GOOD, WHAT IS RIGHT, AND WHAT WE KNOW WE SHOULD DO. BUT IT'S EASY TO 'DRIFT' OFF THE LINE OF BEING PREPARED AND BEING IN POSITION FOR WHAT IS NEXT." CHASE BREAKS THIS DOWN BEAUTIFULLY IN HIS RESPONSE ABOUT HIS NFL DEBUT.

"I'm built from extraordinary commitment towards my craft. And that is where my confidence came from. And if you didn't commit, you start to lack, and you get put in positions to

perform, and you haven't been doing the things that you expect of yourself or remember from yourself from that level of commitment on how you be great, then you start getting ordinary results. And that is really what I have seen happen in that 'drift,' as you call it."

— Chase Minnifield

Chase: I will say, from my three years in pro football, if you see my level of weekly commitment towards being prepared to play at my highest level, it was slowly declining. Because I wasn't seeing my commitment level to the game. And then, even when I was pulled up off the practice squad, you want to get to 53 travel players, but they only dress 46 team members per game. So even then, when you're preparing for the games and playing for anything that may come up, they do not give you a T-shirt.

At that period, when I got called up to dress for my first NFL game, it was midweek. And I think an important point in this situation is the fact that you don't get to choose when you get your opportunity. You do not get to choose. When it is time to go, it is time to go. And that could be an hour before, three days before, five days before, or seven days before. But if I had been told I am starting this week on Monday, going into that next Sunday, then I would have had a different outcome. But I got told late Wednesday, and I've gone Monday, Tuesday, and Wednesday on Scout team. I've missed three days of preparation for the week. So now I am trying to fit a Thursday, Friday, Saturday cram into what I would prepare for a seven-day week. And in that space, it is just because of a drift.

Every week I figured people were playing my position that was not up to par. I believed that I could play the position better, so I stayed ready for up to a year and a half working out at a high intensity level. I do not know how to work out any other way. I can't go in there and jump on the elliptical, I work out high intensity, that's just my makeup in general."

(continued)

(*continued*)

CHASE CREATED A FABULOUS COMPANY AFTER HIS NFL CAREER ENDED, CUT SHORT BY INJURY, A COMMON FACTOR FOR MANY IN PURSUIT OF THE PROFESSIONAL FOOTBALL CAREER PATH. CHASE DISCUSSED HOW HE LEARNED TO CREATE GOOD TEAMS AND MEET THEM RIGHT WHERE THEY ARE ON THEIR JOURNEY AND WITH WHAT THEY CAN CONTRIBUTE. HE IS LOOKING TO PROVE THE STEREOTYPES OF SILICON VALLEY OR TECH INVESTORS INCORRECT AND EXPAND PEOPLE'S THINKING ON WHERE TECH TALENT CAN BE FOUND. CHASE'S WORDS ON THAT REVEAL A SECRET SAUCE HE LEARNED FROM HIS DAYS OF COMPETING AT THE TOP LEVELS OF FOOTBALL.

The business success that we have had today is of a one-percenter, especially coming out of Lexington, Kentucky. With a team that are all in central Kentucky, not too many people have that, and we've had investors tell us left and right, "This isn't going to work." We are invested in this. We hear "no" on a daily basis. And I don't think that's something that most of my team is cut out to handle, but that is what I'm built for. I am built for hearing "no's" and turning those into disbelief or "yes," and that is why I am the leader of the team.

> "In business, I always try to focus on how I can get my mindset for adversity because we're a startup. We are going against billion-dollar corporations, and we are not expected to succeed. We're not expected to succeed in any form or fashion."
> – Chase Minnifield

Not to Be Denied

"Winners, when shown data that they are losing, find a way to win!"

> – Chris McChesney and Sean Covey,
> *The Four Disciplines of Execution*

On my podcast, *Winners Find a Way*, I interview the one-percenters, people who have accomplished what most people never will. They have all gone through trials and discussed how they have learned to overcome challenge. Some challenges are small, while some are larger. As Chase describes going up against the big corporations, he recognizes that he is at a disadvantage for resources. But what athletes recognize quickly as strengths also come with weakness. Most physically large players are strong, but not as quick or fast as smaller players. Can we beat the bigger player through speed? Chase has a small company that is more nimble and can adapt and move quickly. That is a major advantage when the subject is technology. Companies that survive and grow are the ones that stay nimble and adaptive. Or they have the resources to acquire the smaller companies that are innovating so quickly.

Athletes persevere. They are solutions-minded and focused on the elements of achieving success and sustaining it. When faced with challenges, they can quickly adapt and find other ways to compete and not only stay in the game, but ultimately win the game.

The Navy SEALs are a good example of how to operate in small, tactical teams. As a smaller, cohesive unit, they operate with profound striking capabilities with highly trained individuals.

According to an article in *Forbes*, in 2020, the top 1% of workers produce 10% of the output, while the top 5% produce 26% of the output.[1]

Showing Up
Darrell Davies, Head Tennis Referee, US Boys Nationals;
College Tennis Coach (retired)

Coach Davies has been a mentor in my life and a lifelong friend. He was the guy who believed in me when I felt everyone else

(continued)

---

[1]https://www.forbes.com/sites/forbescoachescouncil/2020/01/02/the-cold-hard-truth-behind-how-many-star-employees-you-really-have/

(*continued*)

had either forgotten about me or had given up on me. That may have just been my impression, but he picked me up when I was down and saw the contribution I could make to his team and helped the squad get to the National Championships. We did that together!

TRENT: WHAT ARE KEY QUALITIES YOU STRESSED FOR US TO UNDERSTAND AND QUALITIES YOU WERE LOOKING TO DEVELOP FOR THE PROGRAM FOR SUSTAINABILITY AND LEGACY?

Darrell: Lou Holtz, the famed college football coach, lists four characteristics of winners in one of his books *Wins, Losses and Lessons Learned*. And he did not mean winners win or lose in terms of games all the time, but in life in general. One of his four core principles is perseverance. So as I look back on my life, two things stand out. Perseverance is certainly one of them. The other one is "serendipity." I mean, chance events happen to all of us, but the difference between the impact of those chance events is what you do with them. How do you handle them?

There are some basic ingredients that contribute to success. Lou Holtz said perseverance is one of them. Another one is showing up. Woody Allen said a relevant thing I think, that "90% of success in life is showing up." And that is an important thing when you are teaching. If I have an eight o'clock class in the morning, I have often wondered—why do they show up? They don't have to listen to this lecture, so showing up is critical. Perseverance is critical. Focus is critical. Now you can say "focus," everybody does that for the short term! They're playing tennis, so keep your eye on the ball. What the heck does that really mean? Well, focus, in my opinion, means you keep it simple.

DURING OUR SHOW, I ENJOYED REMINISCING ABOUT WHEN HIS
PROGRAM WAS REAPING ALL THAT HE HAD LEARNED AND WAS A
NATIONALLY RANKED PROGRAM. I WAS A PART OF IT AT THAT
TIME. IT TOOK TIME TO GET THERE. THE COACH SPEAKS ON
BALANCE AND THE KISS PRINCIPLE.

It is interesting to bring balance into the equation. That is the
point and perspective I tried to do with you, Trent, as a player,
and the other players. When I coached, I asked, "Did you do
your best?" We are all gonna have good days and bad days. Everybody does. The best baseball player goes zero for four some
games, right? But I doubt if he goes into the clubhouse thinking
he was a failure that day, or even worse, that it carried over to
the next day. Put your losses behind you. You had a difficult day.

WHEN I PUSHED COACH DAVIES ON THE UNDERLYING THEME
OF PRESSURE, AND WHY IT ENGULFS ATHLETES SOMETIMES,
ESPECIALLY FOR THE INDIVIDUAL SPORTS LIKE TENNIS, WRESTLING, SWIMMING, BOWLING, AND GOLF, FOR EXAMPLE, HIS
RESPONSE WAS TYPICAL OF HIS WHIMSICAL STYLE.

When you think, "I've got to win," it puts pressure on you. If
you can kind of turn that around and say, "Well, I'm not going
to pressure myself to win. I'm going to pressure myself to simply
allow my opponent to lose." The reality of tennis is who really
wins a match? Well, it is the one who hits the ball over the net
the last time, right? I mean, it is pretty simple to talk about. So
those are the kinds of things that I tried to employ. And focusing on positive outcomes as opposed to avoiding negative ones.

And so, one's self talk, if you will, or one's perception of
the moments, the result, the outcome, the day, the tournament, the match. That's important, not only for the moment,
but living with yourself, not tearing yourself apart that day. But

(continued)

> (*continued*)
>
> also, for tomorrow. Even more important for tomorrow, put it behind you.
>
> *"I coach with a KISS method: 'keep it simple, stupid.' And so, simplify things, get down to the basics, the perseverance of showing up, and then realize it's tennis anyway. An important principle that successful players miss some of the time is that you can win a match by simply allowing your opponent to lose."*
> — *Darrell Davies*

Show Up

While I do think there is more to the equation of success than "just showing up," I think Woody Allen has a point. This is how I would adapt the original quote:

> "Show up ready to give all the effort you can, focused on the task at hand, looking to accomplish something, and make whatever you're working on better than it was before you arrived."

Most people are not present or prepared and are distracted. We see these massive errors in transportation, from train wrecks to airplane failures, and over 80% of the mistakes are human error. We trust people with a great deal of responsibility and folks are not rested, they are too caffeine-fueled, stressed, and poorly prepared. Then, on top of that, the many different distractions from phone beeps to regular interruptions are at an all-time high.

We cannot even get smartphones out of our employees' or students' hands when we know it is reducing the amount of information they are taking in and is limiting their productivity. It is also creating numerous unsafe conditions. Statistics from 2021 show that 8–9% of fatalities in driving were caused by distracted driving—more than 3,500 deaths, and injuries caused by distracted driving are over 100 times that. In over 12% of all distracted fatalities, a cellphone was in use. The fatalities caused by the phone are at 17% for teens drivers under 20, 16% for 21–24, and it starts going down slowly. There is a $98 billion direct and indirect cost to the economy. If you are held responsible for a distracted driving accident, your insurance will rise an average of 49%.[2, 3]

Let us get intentional with what we really want to accomplish. You may have to say "no" to some things so that you have the energy and bandwidth to give your absolute best and full attention to what is important to you.

Showing up means being on time, physically, mentally, and emotionally prepared, and with our full attention for the matter at hand.

Grow as People
Bobby Magallanes, 29 Years in Professional Baseball; Atlanta Braves Hitting Coach; Performance Psychologist

Bobby Mags, or Mags as his friends call him, has always been a deep thinker, steeped in patience and faith. He is one of the most grounded people I know. He also is a consistent force in the coaching industry. I had the blessing of coaching alongside Mags for seven seasons with the LA Angels. It was fun and thrilling to invite him on my show after winning a World Championship as a coach for the Atlanta Braves! He put things in my terms as a strength and conditioning coach, and as a person who has also reached the World Series.

(continued)

---

[2]https://www.valuepenguin.com/auto-insurance-distracted-driving-statistics#:~:text=Distracted%20Driving%20Statistics%20%2D%20Crash%20Data%20for%20Texting%20%26%20Cellphone%20Usage&text=Distracted%20driving%20caused%203%2C522%20deaths,caused%20410%20deaths%20that%20year
[3]https://drivethru.gsa.gov/DRIVERSAFETY/DistractedDrivingPosterA.pdf

(*continued*)

Mags received his undergraduate degree in his forties and a master's in performance psychology in his fifties—now that is being dedicated to your craft.

TRENT: LET'S DISCUSS THE PSYCHOLOGY OF PERSEVERANCE AND BECOMING SUCCESSFUL.

Bobby: Sports training is like muscle. For a muscle to grow it has to be torn down and then rebuilt. And then it keeps on tearing and rebuilding for progression.

A lump of coal is the ugliest rock. But that lump of coal, only through consistent pressure and heat, becomes a diamond. Diamonds are the most precious rock! I went through that like no one's business to finally arrive in the major leagues, which I praise God about, but it is not easy, and it means going through a lot, but that's what shapes us. That is what forms us, and that is what prepares us to get to that moment.

"Well, that's how we are as people. It is like we got to kind of be torn down a little bit to keep growing and getting better and that's how our faith grows and that's how we grow as people."
— *Bobby Magallanes*

Pressure over Time

Athletes get trained, broken down, and then built back up. I always feel like we're making diamonds—a precious stone shaped by pressure and time. It takes foresight and skill to see what potential can look like in people. I find it important and necessary for people to lean into their God-given strengths to become what they were meant for and likely made for.

I always thought as a kid I would be an NFL player. I liked playing and my dad was my coach, so I got to spend time with him, and I enjoyed scoring touchdowns because I was fast. But by age 12 or 13, kids were growing faster than me. I was behind on the growth curve, and my parents were five-foot-six and five-foot-three. In fact, I could not recall a single person on either side of the family who was over six feet tall. I recall being super excited that one of my cousins was married to a tall guy (probably six-foot-one) but I then learned he is not part of the bloodline, taking more wind out of my sails on how tall I likely would be.

So after breaking my leg in a football game in seventh grade, I realized that maybe the NFL was not in my future. I still enjoyed the sport, but I had to come to terms with my strengths and for what I was made. If I stood next to the players in Major League Baseball, I would still not fit in, unless I was standing next to Jose Altuve of the Houston Astros. (So there are exceptions to the rule.)

One of the key elements of pressure is that, I believe, it is self-applied. I choose which pressures I let in; and some are warranted and some are not. I have applied pressure to myself to finalize and finish this book. It is important to me. I put pressure on myself to be prepared to speak in front of audiences because we only get a few opportunities to touch lives and I am thankful for them. But if a client somewhere wants to try to apply pressure on getting an assignment completed that I do not find important or urgent, I do not have to allow that in. The pressure remains a choice. An emergency on your part does not constitute an emergency for me.

For my mentors, I have always put a great deal of pressure on myself to deliver for them and bring my A game when it comes to our meetings. It is an opportunity to improve myself and my company, and I will not choose to miss that. Also, out of respect for the mentor and their willingness to volunteer their time, I want to assure we both maximize value.

Every person has the same 24 hours each day. The adage "Rome was not built in a day" is pertinent to what we are going for. Microsoft founder Bill Gates said, "We overestimate what we can accomplish in one year, and underestimate what we can accomplish in 10 years." Use your minutes and hours well.

If you are thinking big—and I know you are because you're reading this book—it takes time to form the diamond. Be forthright and focused, but with patience and perseverance.

Be Relentless

Shanna Dickerson, Gymnast; Tennis
Player; Owner, Blue Sky Luxury Travel

When I sat down with Shanna, I had no idea she was once an Olympic hopeful in gymnastics. I know she is a fabulous tennis player, a sport for which we share a love. I welcomed her to *Winners Find a Way* as a 1% entrepreneur in the highly competitive luxury-class travel business, and our networks cross over because of the services her company provides. Her clients are the one-percenters, and she must be aware of their desires, needs, and demands. Folks in her network expect the best experiences and do not compromise.

TRENT: TELL ME ABOUT CREATING A DYNAMIC TEAM TO COMPETE WITH A POPULATION THAT WANTS PERFECTION EVERY TIME—AND ARE WILLING TO PAY FOR IT. HOW DO YOU COMPETE, GET AHEAD, AND HOW DO YOU KEEP YOUR SANITY?

Shanna: I am relentless, as you can imagine, relentless. If I truly believe in something, or a project or someone or whatever, and someone tells me no, then I'm going back in again. You just gave me one no, but I'm going to keep going. And I think as an entrepreneur, it's just something that if you're really all in, you're relentless. And I do not meet a whole lot of people that are, plus I'm a Virgo. So I'm a Virgo business, which means work crazy, be relentless. And I think you have to have that in the business world.

I would say one of the best things I ever did for my psyche, so to speak, is to learn meditation. I started doing it in 2015 and have done it almost daily since. And I think that if you can be super happy and content on the inside, then everything is going to be okay. I think kindness and just being a responsible and respectful businessperson is how I sleep at night.

When someone hands you an amazing opportunity, and you do not know how to do it, you say yes, and then you figure it out later. I'm learning as I go and it's extremely difficult, that part, but it's okay, we'll figure it out. So you just say yes, and you figure it out.

I think Oprah has said this quite a bit: If an opportunity or if something in your life, your biggest shot knocks, and the door closes, whatever it is, I promise there is a reason for it. I fully believe in the universe that there is a better thing or direction that you are supposed to take, and you and I might just trust in the universe. I know that sounds a little corny and meditation-like, or whatever.

"I am relentless, as you can imagine, relentless."
— *Shanna Dickerson*

Resolute or Delusional

I am an encourager at heart, and I want everyone around me to succeed. I also surround myself with brave souls who take big risks and win often, but they lose too. If there are going to be games to be played, there will be winners and losers. But I live by the mantra "You win, or you learn." The only real loss is if you do not receive the lesson of that journey.

As you dedicate yourself to what you are striving for and doing, keep a team of key personnel near you, like an advisory board. When you have mentors around you who have done what you are looking to accomplish, they will be instrumental in helping you stay focused on what you need to start doing more of and, equally important, what you need to stop doing.

The other key elements of this team will be to vet your SMAART goals:

- Getting **specific** will help you recruit the right teammates and the right customers too.
- Measurements are supposed to help keep the goal moving and **measure** the value of something that will allow us to know we are heading in the direction of winning.

- **Attainable** becomes an insight that sometimes only the right advisory team can speak too. If I had asked my advisors if I should dedicate myself to be the best "little big man" in the NBA and start training to play in the post, they would have told me I was delusional. Someone must tell it to you straight.
- **Aligned** is a component often overlooked in goal setting. Our goals should align with our values and the mission of the journey and business. If those are working in conflict with each other, this is likely a poor goal. Even if it is a personal goal, it should still align with your values.
- Having a **realistic** goal helps us not underestimate or overestimate what we are going for.
- This advisory team should push and stretch your goals in a certain **time**, but no one should be looking to accomplish a three-year plan in 12 months and expect a great deal of success.

Key Takeaways

- Be prepared, apply consistent effort, and be adaptable to seize unexpected opportunities.
- Continuous improvement, focus, and dedication are essential for sustained success.
- Be nimble when competing against larger organizations.
- Perseverance is necessary to achieve success.
- Pressure is self-applied.
- Show up mentally and emotionally prepared, stay fully focused, and give maximum effort.
- Work with mentors who are aligned with your values to reach your full potential.
- Persistence, learning from challenges, and kindness in business is necessary in any entrepreneurial endeavor.

- Set goals that are specific, measurable, and attainable, that are aligned with values, realistic, and time-bound, and are vetted by an advisory team.
- Build an advisory board with advocates offering tough love and support.

The Pain Exchange

Help yourself through hyper-learning and build a team around you that will support you and be your biggest advocate. Do not choose "yes" folks for your team who will not push you to reach your potential. Make sure that while each advocate wants to see you succeed, they are willing to give you the "tough love" you need to reach your full potential, as well as your team members and the business itself.

Start by creating a list of potential advocates. Consider three to five people who could help you achieve and get to the next level. Find the top three to five people who have created the most value and ask them for help. Pick wisely. I encourage you to shoot for the stars on these asks. Be prepared to stretch yourself by having uncomfortable conversations with industry titans. Here are my thoughts on the people you may choose to be a part of your advisory team:

- A person who is a value-based businessperson who can help you achieve your business objectives, while fully being aligned with the same values you have for yourself and your team members. This is a watchdog role.
- Someone who is a specialist in an area that you lack the most. This is often an accountant or lawyer, or someone else in the professional services who has a level of skill that is needed in your industry and without them often will result in players losing because of their lack of knowledge and inexperience in this area. This will shore up a major gap in your team very quickly.

- Another person would be an outside-the-box thinker and strategic risk taker who will push you to play at levels you have not had the courage to play at and change the course of thinking to create real value through innovation—a 10-times thinker with real-world experience doing it.
- A final person could be a stabilizer, a conservative thinker who must be convinced of the value of everything, has your best interest at heart, and can argue a point.

Each member of your advisory board must check their ego at the door and come in bringing their business knowledge and efforts. Meetings can be monthly, every other month, or, at a minimum, quarterly. Compensation could be in stock, a small stipend, T&E with a good visit to a desired location, or a nice holiday card or gift at Thanksgiving or Christmas. Get folks at the top, because the better the network of each of these folks, the more they will value the meetings. Then they do not just come for you, but the chance to spend time with fellow one-percenters!

12

Conflict and the Rules of Engagement

ONE OF THE differences between conflict in a business and conflict that may occur in professional sports is the intensity. That is not to say that conflict is not happening everywhere and that it's not intense. We have seen workplace violence since the beginning of time, and we also know that there is plenty of conflict regularly occurring in most of our lives at some level.

Disagreements, challenges, and conflict are a few of the primary reasons why people work every day. It is why people have roles in organizations: to solve issues and complex challenges. They are the people with training called on to resolve issues through their sense of ethics, skills, training, logic, and more.

A Threat of Violence

The reality is that the threat of violence in sports is much higher among men. I had not really considered it, but when I heard Dr. Jordan Peterson discuss conflict in an interview, I was stunned when he talked about the ever-present underlying current and threat of violence when conflict arrives among men versus women. Conflict shows up in many ways and begins in ridiculously small terms, such as embarrassment, snarky comments, gossiping behind someone's back, water cooler disagreements, sarcasm, or debates, often indirect to the conflicting parties but passively aggressive.

Direct challengers are often seen as overaggressive and "problems" in an organization. This has always challenged my thinking because I am not sure I understand what the measures are of good versus unruly, acceptable versus unacceptable behavior. If you are spreading a cancerous message of discord against the alignment of the leadership inside your organization, that is seen as not great, but nonaggressive and more passive, and thus permissible. But if you confront the person or leader who is the source of the information and question the fabric of the decision and request open debate, you are seen as an aggressive troublemaker, looking for a fight—not permissible.

Fighting in hockey is a form of discipline and part of the inner code of the sport for rules of engagement. There are rules that are established inside the parameters of a hockey team, the game itself, and the actual rules of the game. But many things happen outside of the "official" hockey rules. People like to see the game of hockey because of the accepted fighting and violence that can occur. It's considered entertaining. Hockey is a regulated structure through rules of engagement. And people get to watch it play out in real time, though many of the rules of the team are more internal but can still play out similarly to the public arena and viewing. Matters are often managed "internally."

Violence is not an accepted form of conflict in business environments. But the same poor behaviors are still showing up and the challenges are similar and real. Yet the engagement can and should be a more controlled environment and one of professionalism, which can be much more civil than the physical threats and strengths of world-class sports, which already likely have a touch of violence in the sport itself.

Trust Equals Productive Conflict

"Conflict is the pursuit of truth. When team members trust each other and know that everyone is capable of admitting when they're wrong, then conflict becomes nothing more than the pursuit of truth or the best possible answer."

– Patrick Lencioni, *The Five Behaviors of a Cohesive Team*

As we look back to Chapter 3 on great teams, the *team* foundation is built on trust. If we trust one another, then any conflict becomes a unified search for truth and the best answer. When we don't trust, conflict arises on whose ideas get credit, how I might look coming out of this disagreement, will I be reprimanded for questioning the logic of the decision, and many other selfish or agenda-based concepts arise. This is important to get right at the onset.

Most organizations do not have consistent, stated rules of engagement for conflict. I find this an abhorrent mistake. Every organization is going to have conflict. It's what most people are hired to manage, though few will put that in any open advertisement for a position. But the truth of the matter is that skilled professionals are hired to manage challenging and demanding situations and events, utilizing their experience, training, and skill sets.

Conflict and Generational Gaps

Nicole Donnelly, Marketing Expert; Entrepreneur; Pro Snowboarder (retired)

When Nicole joined me on *Winners Find a Way*, I tapped into her former pro snowboarder journey in the early days of ESPN's *The X Games*, and how that helped her transition to be a business owner. The following is some of our conversation where

(*continued*)

(*continued*)

Nicole talked about how she approaches adversity, first through her "determined" attitude and then her view on her abilities:

"I know that I will, and I'm determined to find a way. And so, I just keep seeking and finding a way because if you think of it, like a little kid, I'm gonna get my way. And I'm gonna find out how to do it. And I have that same drive and determination, whether it is snowboarding, business, or whatever. I'm gonna find a way to get there."

— *Nicole Donnelly*

TRENT: AT AN EARLY AGE YOU WERE DEEMED A SNOWBOARDING TALENT AND HAD TO DECIDE TO "GO FOR IT" AND COMPETE ON AN EARLY STAGE SNOWBOARDING PRO TOUR. PEOPLE MAY NOT REALIZE THIS MEANS GOING INTO SOME OF THE MOST EXPENSIVE RESORT TOWNS IN THE WORLD AND HAVING TO "MAKE YOUR WAY" LONG BEFORE THE BIG SPONSORSHIP DOLLARS OF TODAY'S X GAMES. A LOT OF SACRIFICES FOR MERE COMFORTS ARE MADE. WHAT DID THE EXPERIENCE OF SLEEPING IN YOUR CAR IN A COLORADO MOUNTAIN TOWN BEFORE HEADING INTO COMPETITION AGAINST THE BEST IN THE WORLD TEACH YOU?

Nicole: I have self-confidence and belief in myself, I guess. That I can do the things that I want to, and it's been a matter of figuring out what I want to put my energy behind. Because whatever it is, I'll figure it out.

In business, it could be getting press and getting on big shows. It could be for my new podcast and getting some big guests. However, I'm determined to get what I want to get to that point, to get to that contact, and I don't stop asking. I ask for help. I ask other people, "Do you know somebody who knows this person," or whatever it is. When I want something, I just cannot stop that drive.

THERE ARE LOTS OF GAPS AND DIFFERENCES IN HOW PEOPLE SHOW UP FROM THEIR DIFFERENT ERAS, AND THEIR UPBRINGING IN THOSE TIMES OF THEIR GENERATION. YOU AUTHORED A BOOK ON THE EMOTIONAL INTELLIGENCE ASPECT OF DEALING WITH ADVERSITY AND POSITIVE REINFORCEMENT. WHAT WERE A COUPLE OF BIG TAKEAWAYS?

The *Happy Camper Guidebook* that I wrote talks about the six basic emotional needs, and everybody has needs that are a little different. And the way that you are talking about it is very typical Gen X and generational. Millennials are different. The different generations expect a different type of leadership. And the Millennial generation is more cooperative and tell each other they are doing an excellent job. And Xers are like latch-key kids. They're like, "I didn't get it, so you're not going to get it." I think my statement was of the Gen X kind of a mindset.

A Conflict Wrench

Nicole Donnelly has run the half-pipe on mountains all over the world and ran businesses with labor in both the US and Canada. She brings a new light on conflict: generational differences. Let us add to our interpretations of what conflict looks like and how differing levels of consequences play in our interpretations of how things should be overseen. Not only those things, but bring in economic factors, geography, cultural norms, eras in time, and many more.

This "wrench" that is being thrown in on all our own interpretations leaves us with varying thoughts and remedies to conflict. This is why setting rules and boundaries are so important. In fact, I consider it irresponsible for organizations not to have established rules and roles and how the effectiveness of the chain of command and organizational charts become important in having productive conflict across an organization.

The Other Side of Fear

Victoria Pelletier, Former Hockey Player; COO at Age 24

Victoria has been a leader from the beginning, coming right out of school as an athlete and type-A personality. We are cut from the same cloth of competitiveness and work to lead by anticipating the next challenge before it arrives.

What most people do not know about Victoria is what created her drive and her lived experience of being the daughter of a drug-addicted 16-year-old mother. Her adopted parents saved her from a life of abuse and pulled her from a situation that she might not have survived otherwise.

She has been tapped on the shoulder to lead from the very beginning of her professional career because she learned how to channel that deep desire to be loved and valued, and lead from example with no excuses.

She went through over 18 mergers and acquisitions in business. The M&A environment is fierce, and Victoria must take on her business persona and balance that versus her personal family dynamic and persona.

As Victoria joined *Winners Find a Way*, I asked her about moving forward past her history getting mired in a "woe is me" attitude, but she has never taken that approach.

"Circumstances of our past should not rob us of our future."
— *Victoria Pelletier*

TRENT: WHAT DID PEOPLE RECOGNIZE IN YOU AT THAT NOTICEABLY YOUTHFUL AGE AND WHAT HELPED SEPARATE YOU FROM OTHERS?

Victoria: I am going to not only take action, but I will model the thinking, the language, and the behavior I need to go forward. And so that is the choice I have. So my children hate that. I'm like, no excuses. But it is really that we have choices and that is why there is no victimhood here with me.

How have your own convictions shaped your future vision and how can you accomplish more?

I am a big believer in convictions. I don't like people asking me, "How do you have it all?" Like, how can you "have it all," while making excuses for their inability to do other things? For me, I say where there's conviction, there is capacity. So if you truly believe in it, you want to do it.

And then also, I'll say, you get particularly good at saying no to the things that don't bring your personal or professional life joy or value.

Say no or delegate or outsource things you really don't get energy from. Barter, gig work, and get creative using resources to make things work. There are solutions!

You grew up in a tough environment, and you were so driven to get out of that environment and prove to everyone that you could get out. How did you manage that and other people?

It used to fuel me to say, "I'm going to prove you all wrong, I am getting out of here. And I am going to strive for something better." I never once leveraged where I came from, at all, and the circumstance and challenge that I had. I use it to fuel me, I did not use it to gain advantage in the workplace or beyond that.

I tell my team members, "There are no schedules, there are just deliverables." I inherently trust my team members.

(*continued*)

(*continued*)

IS THERE A GO-TO READING OR QUOTE THAT CAN LEVEL YOU
AND GET YOU BACK TO FOCUS WHEN YOU ARE LOSING, OR DOWN?

My favorite quote is on my wall in my office, by George Addair: "Everything you've ever wanted lives on the other side of fear."

"And for me, there is no excuse in that we have a choice in terms of how we are going to move forward. Where there is conviction, there is capacity."

– Victoria Pelletier

No Victimhood

I like Victoria's stance on "no excuses." And I am sure that sounds harsh sometimes, but as stated earlier, it is a losing behavior that will not amount to much. As I covered in the Quadrant of Death in Chapter 8, Jeremy Spann has a fixed rule of no excuses and no apologies. His premise is that if you have the time to think of an excuse or must return a call or go to someone to apologize, you likely have time to fix it! I like his theory, though I might not fully agree with the apology part.

I believe people falter, make errors, and can make poor decisions. I expect, from both myself and those closest to us, three key things to a worthy apology—and they are absolutely necessary at times:

1. Take responsibility and state the infraction and your role in it with clarity and specificity.

2. Tell the person you are sorry with an authentic and genuine spirit knowing in your heart you are sorry.

3. Ask that person for forgiveness.

Being specific on your part and taking responsibility shows true understanding of the infraction. Being authentic about it says that you have considered the pain that may have been caused and you care about their well-being. And asking for forgiveness is a step to mending the relationship, though you should know that if the infraction is significant enough, it may not be granted. Expect that sometimes it may take another person time to fully feel that forgiveness in their heart and be able to grant it. It may take days, weeks, or months. If it takes years, someone is harboring it and now shoulders guilt.

Work diligently through any trespass so that you can know that forgiveness in your heart.

"Resentment is like drinking poison and waiting for the other person to die."

– Saint Augustine

No Autopsy in the Street

When conflict arises—and it will—we must have a plan. When a horrific accident happens and someone has died from an injury or accident, a coroner is called. There are clear rules of preservation and respect for the dead. Investigators stay on the scene, but the body is removed quickly. There is no autopsy at the scene of the accident! That is not part of the protocol. These rules around the deceased are both civil and sometimes critical to determining what exactly happened.

If your rules are out of order, crazy things happen, and people take liberties in conflict. We see this play out in numerous bad behaviors within an organization. First, conflict is not first nature to most people. We are looking to eliminate or avoid it often, so it is already uncomfortable. When we are not comfortable and emotionally charged, bad decisions are made. We do not have the repetitions or preparation often to do conflict well, so our confidence in our abilities is limited. Second, when a lack of rules exists, they are left up to interpretation and often seem more "made up as we go." This happens when there is no training, poor skills, a lack of

successful experiences, and team members will make their own procedures that may not align with the company.

Moderate the Mission

As a leader who is required to help others work through conflict and
do that in a healthy way, I believe it is important to stay focused and
committed to the greater team goal and mission. Understand the
dynamic of the conflict and follow your organization's guidelines
and values. Model the guided behaviors in all your interactions
with others so that team members know what successful and what
productive conflict can look like.

Rise to the Top

I dare say that the organization that has healthy and productive
conflict will rise to the top quickly in their industry because of the
inherent established internal organization and trust this team must
have to get the result. Plus, the inefficiency of dealing with
unhealthy conflict is the big deterrent and loss of focus to every
organization that immediately causes a drop in productivity versus
the competition. Why would any organization and team want to
spend their quality energy in this area?

Key Takeaways

- Establish important rules and unacceptable behaviors.
- Trust transforms conflict into a pursuit of truth.
- Create clear guidelines and consistent rules for conflict
  engagement.
- Understand generational gaps influencing conflict management.
- Our next challenge will lead to a better solution.
- Avoiding victimhood, embracing convictions, and taking
  responsibility is crucial in leadership.

- A worthy apology involves taking responsibility, expressing genuine remorse, apologizing, and seeking forgiveness.
- Organizations with healthy conflict resolution mechanisms outperform competitors due to enhanced focus, trust, efficiency, and productivity.

The Pain Exchange

Create rules of engagement for your team, household, and/or organization.

Operating through a clear plan for conflict and rules of engagement should be a part of every organization's handbook and provide clarity for best practices around conflict. This will alleviate tons of issues and challenges among team members, plus lower the risk of bad behavior and inefficiencies due to loss of focus, HR issues, reprimand, culture challenges, sides taken, and more.

Start with a list of standard steps to take when conflict arises. Most of these steps are non-negotiable. Here are 10 ideas to consider, from Joyce Marter:

1. Pause and get grounded (check in on emotions first).
2. Zoom out to gain perspective (remove emotions and view from 10,000 feet).
3. Be mindful of nonverbal communication (intensity, facial, hand gestures, etc.).
4. Avoid behaviors that add fuel to the fire:
   o Criticism
   o Contempt
   o Stonewalling
   o Defensiveness
5. Reflect empathy (e.g., "I've heard it before," "You are not alone").
6. Take responsibility for yourself (ownership of your own poor behavior and choices).

7. Use of assertive communication (in-person):
   o Avoid passive, aggressive, or passive-aggressive behaviors.
   o Stay in the present.
   o Use "I" statements, rather than "you" statements.

8. Be open and flexible.

9. Focus on what you can control and let go of the rest (how you react).

10. Forgive.

Take inventory before addressing the conflict of how you are choosing to show up and conduct yourself and behave through both verbal and nonverbal communication:

- Assessing your attitude is one of trust for the organization and the team members involved.
- Reflecting clarity, your messaging should be focused only on facts, not assumptions, hearsay, history, or emotions.
- Be ready to be an active listener with an intention to understand the other person's intentions and perspectives.
- Words matter. Do not be snarky, judgmental, harsh, standoffish, aggressive, nonresponsive, or fail to engage.
- Be focused and keep timing and rules of engagement so all parties are heard and listened to.

Advanced Pain Exchange

If conflict becomes anger, here are useful tips to consider for mediating team members through challenges. Anger is likely to escalate to something physical, or a poor emotional condition. Diffuse this quickly and never let it fester. A plan for this level of conflict is necessary.

I like to remind myself that while I do not love anger, I respect the passion it takes to get to this point because I always assume that the person actually cares enough to get to this level. Here are suggestions from Dr. David Clarke:

1. Cease fire
   - Everyone falls back.
   - Take a breath and allotted time to calm down and take consideration.
   - Meditate privately—deep breaths; calm the body and mind.

2. The right time and place (choose wisely)
   - Private
   - Quiet
   - Comfortable

3. One at a time
   - One person (first) speaks for no more than 10 minutes.
   - All others are active listeners, listening to understand.
   - Take a break.
   - Second person speaks for no more than 10 minutes.
   - All others are active listeners, listening to understand.
   - Take a break (three-quarters done!).

4. Processing (later the same day or next day)
   - Gather in conflict space (see above).
   - Repeat step 3 with what we learned.
   - Seek understanding and resolution. (Note that understanding does *not* equal agreement.)
   - Take a break for "Let's Make a Deal":

     Mediate to get closure.

     Define go-forward.

     Compromise from both sides.

     Negotiate.

     Decisions are not final and can be amended if not working (scrap and reset).

Tips
   - Take it slowly; two days or more to resolve an angry or challenging conflict is not abnormal.

- Stop and start, *as many times as necessary*. Emotions ramp up, or boil over, *stop*. Take a 30-minute caucus—meditate, eat, pray, walk, listen to music, level the system, and be emotionally prepared to get back to active listening and delivering messages with clarity. (But see warning below.)
- Keep the bigger mission of the organization at the forefront of the conflict to assure we are battling out something that truly matters to the mission.
- Build ground rules, rules of engagement, and standard conduct policies in advance.
- Practice, practice, practice.

Warning: If stops and starts continue with the same person on multiple occasions in which the person is consistently behaving badly, unprofessional, and outside the agreement of our rules of engagement, here is my management of such an individual. I will send a warning after each infraction on the above rules of engagement during the subsequent stop. After two warnings, on the third stop I will let the person know privately that the behavior is unacceptable and unprofessional and will no longer be tolerated in our discussions. I will often summon a longer break, likely overnight and a chance to "sleep on it." Then I begin the final meeting with a final warning that if any of the rules are not followed or any unbecoming and unacceptable behavior is shown again, that person will have eliminated themselves from the conflict solution. And then the remaining interviews will be completed, and decisions will be made on the premises of understanding on the information that we have, and that person will no longer be allowed to participate in the process. Their full compliance with whatever solution and decision made will be fully expected to be met with acceptance, and they should be prepared to move forward with the team as a unit based on whatever decisions are made. They have lost the right to be a part of the solution.

13

Never Stop Learning—and the Art of Continuous Improvement

ONE THING THAT most people don't know about me is that I received a teaching degree from the University of Toledo. I did not end up choosing the path of the traditional grade school teacher and coach. But learning and teaching has been in my professional DNA, when I started teaching tennis to kids when I was 16 years old, and before that, instructing my paper route part-time employees when I was 12.

Levels of Learning

It has been a journey of continuous learning and hyper-learning with fellow professional athletes early in my professional career, to the top 3% of business owners globally, and from the Entrepreneurs' Organization.

From the time I left university, I was submerged in two valuable lessons on learning. First, if I was unable to learn fast, I would never survive in professional baseball. Because the learning is at such a high intensity, you are being trained to learn in a very kinesthetic way. This is one of the three learning styles: auditory (humans have been learning this way for millennia), visual (our main style of learning in our schools), and kinesthetic (see Figure 13.1). Kinesthetic learning is an active way of learning through discussions,

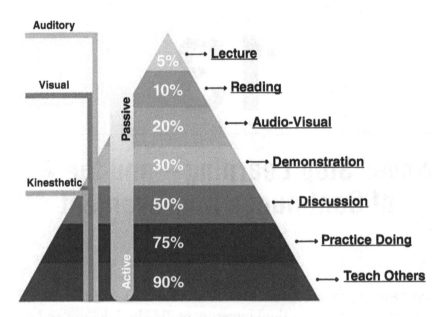

Figure 13.1   The Learning Retention Pyramid.

physical practice, and then the opportunity to teach others the skills we have learned (highest levels of retention rate).

The second lesson is that having the skills to adapt to another skill quickly, and be as effective doing it, is crucial to your success. Often organizations ask their teams to pivot and adapt to a different skill or strategy, which means new skills are needed, and you must be equally proficient at them. Plus, get the results. The challenge is that most people become highly skilled in one area, but not in another. They either do not have the ability to adapt or have not been trained in the skill that the organization is asking them to adapt to.

I'll Know You Know It When You Can Teach It

We have learned the best way to retain information is to teach someone else what you have learned. Most instructors are considered experts in passing along knowledge. What we have learned is the way to teach others is crucial, and passive learning styles have extraordinarily little retention rates.

It's funny to me that our "higher learning" institutions and the universities of the world—supposed experts in learning and training, and the most expensive learning in the world—utilize the lowest retention rate model possible. Does anyone else find that ironic?

I have watched my children go on church retreats and have been immersed in learning for a long weekend, or summer camp for a week, and the amount of learning in an abbreviated time is quite miraculous. I have found this same thing in the mission field as well. The active levels of learning and kinesthetic style far outweigh our retention rates versus the passive counterparts.

Retention Rates Equals Coachability

If you ever head to a Major League Baseball Spring Training and are blessed to have inside access, the days are long and full of learning through a blend of all three styles of learning, but the kinesthetic style is on full display. Physical work alongside a coach is what separates athletes from their counterparts in the work and business world. *One of the established superpowers of athletes is hyper-learning and an ability to ramp retention rates to a massive level.*

One of the biggest attributes of our go-to team members is coachability. But when looking at this at a deeper level, they are typically team members who have extremely elevated levels of retention rates and an ability to balance tasks with precision for prioritization.

Open to Learn

Mark Shapiro, MLB Team President; CEO, Toronto Blue Jays and Cleveland Indians

I had the pleasure of working with Mark back in the mid-1990s with the Cleveland Indians, learning very quickly and diligently to stay ahead of the competition. Mark led a core player development team that was regularly rewarded for being the top organization in baseball.

(continued)

(*continued*)

Mark was instrumental in bringing the IEP, or individualized education plan, to professional baseball. Having come directly out of one of the top physical education programs in the country at the University of Toledo, the Cleveland Indians and Mark intrigued me because it was clear that this style of learning the Indians were imposing felt foreign to others looking in. But I knew exactly the intent and the level of effectiveness it would have—making individuals accountable and leveraging their learning to produce better individual productivity that was being clearly measured.

Ultimately, the plan was to make both the individual and the team better. It moved Cleveland from being an organization consistently ranked in the bottom 10%, and the feature of a movie, *Major League*, highlighting the lowlights of the franchise, to regularly competing for the World Series title.

Mark was directly involved in that turnaround for the storied franchise, and it was a massive effort of having a heck of a lot of the "right" players in place. But Dick Jacobs, the owner at the time, clearly had a vision for the future of his organization that turned rapidly from 1990, when they were improving but 11 games out of first, to 1994, when the Indians were 1 game back from first place when the MLB strike extended their 40-year playoff drought. Forty years!

Mark and I have remained friends for over 20 years, and as I began working on a book to discuss high achievement, he was the right guy to call—a lifelong learner who continues to adapt and learn as the President of the Toronto Blue Jays.

My first question was around being a good high school football player, which launched a collegiate playing career at Princeton.

TRENT: WHAT DID YOU LEARN FROM THOSE FORMIDABLE DAYS AND WHICH PEOPLE HAD THE MOST IMPACT ON YOU?

Mark: I think the people that impacted me are more my high school coaches, in particular my head coach and so many things about him that I've expressed to him along the way, particularly the perseverance and determination and how that would help me outlast and beat so many people just by not giving up, and not giving in. The understanding was that I had the ability to do things beyond what I thought was possible physically by outworking people.

Football just provided so many great windows into that. And frankly my experience in college was one more of dealing with something that was not what I expected it to be, to go from such an ideal setting in high school to one where we clearly started to be more of a business. And the relationship with the coaches was vastly different and not quite as personal and not quite as maybe authentic, or sincere. So having to deal with maybe both some disappointment and then just how you respond to that and understanding that even within challenges and setbacks and this would become a common thread to my belief in athletes and executives and people in life—that the mindset of approaching setbacks and challenges are opportunities to grow, learn, and develop is an absolute separator.

WHAT WAS ONE OF THE MOST IMPORTANT LESSONS ALONG THE WAY AND DO YOU MODEL YOUR LEADERSHIP STYLE AFTER ONE OF YOUR FORMER COACHES?

I'm not a big believer that any one person should be the model. I think you take bits and pieces from everyone. And I think you must have one thing that we have not mentioned to date; that would be humility. And so I think you approach every day with humility. It's essential that you have an openness to learn.

(*continued*)

(continued)

And so that openness to learn can come from learning from leaders but it can also come from an intern. I have taken probably thousands of different things from hundreds of different people. A lot of different people have shaped who I am and that is a work in progress, because I think there is an opportunity for me to get better every single day. And when I stop feeling that it is probably time to stop leading people.

YOU HAVE HAD TONS OF FABULOUS COACHES AND EXECUTIVES WHO HAVE SURROUNDED YOU FOR YEARS. DOES ONE STICK OUT AS UNDERSTANDING AND MODELING THE "OPENNESS TO LEARNING" CONCEPT?

I think any culture that I am a part of, it is one of the absolute mandates, and maybe the person I learned this from is the best, Terry Francona (Tito, for those who know him). It is an understanding, that "Hey, we don't have that all figured out and if we don't wake up thinking about how we can get better than someone is going to pass us by." And Tito is a guy who came into Cleveland having won two World Championships, broken the curse in Boston, and clearly could have walked in and commanded enough respect to act as if he had it all figured out and he just commanded the room and commanded his staff.

Instead, the tone he set from the day he got to Cleveland was one of humility, one of openness to learning, one that I think is so powerful because the openness wasn't just to learn from senior executives it was, "Hey, if there's an intern that has good advice for me about bullpen usage or line up construction, I'm listening because I want to get better and I don't really discriminate on where that good information comes from as long as it comes." And so I think Tito, for me, was one guy who certainly modeled that and that made a substantial impact.

> You have been tagged as an inclusive leader who treats his staff and team members with the utmost respect, but that goes deeper for you. Who had the most influence on you as a leader?
>
> *"I mean the biggest influences for me start with my father and that's about how you treat people. And I think that is a thread that runs through everything I believe in leadership and culture. He treated the custodian the same way he treated the mayor of Baltimore. He never qualified people and consistently demonstrated compassion and respect."*
>
> *– Mark Shapiro*

Wide Open

An open mind will get you somewhere. Humility will get you everywhere. Humble people are approachable and inclusive to others. The biggest trait is that learning will never stop from a humble person because it is never focused as a "me first" attitude.

If folks who are leading others recognize the responsibility to be their best for their team members, they are wide open to learning and the radar is consistently on and up to seek that learning that is available to them, all the time, and sometimes that learning will come from the most unlikely sources. Modeling a consistent level of coachability, retention, desire to learn, and continuous improvement is what makes the top leaders.

> ### Pressure Is Self-Applied
> Matt Mieske, MLB Player: Cubs, Brewers, Angels, Mariners; Certified Financial Planner; Entrepreneur
>
> Matt and I got to know one another late in his career as he signed with us in Anaheim as an MLB journeyman outfielder.
>
> *(continued)*

(*continued*)

And I knew of him growing up, having both played baseball in high school in Michigan and at rival colleges in the Mid-American Conference.

Then Matt turned out to be a neighbor of mine in Arizona and a fellow member at our church. Our relationship developed more after his playing career and at the end of my coaching career. He still invests my children's 529 college funds and we have known each other for over 20 years.

I welcomed Matt to *Winners Find a Way* in 2021.

TRENT: WHAT DID YOU LEARN FROM A TIME IN YOUR LIFE WHEN YOU WERE NOT SUCCESSFUL AND FACED FAILURE, AND HOW DID YOU OVERCOME THAT?

Matt: In the minors, in AAA, I was pressing harder and harder and you're one step away. You want to succeed so much and get there that the results were just diminishing. I was just burying myself further into almost a depression really. It was a failure for me. It never happened in any sport or anything academic, nothing, and now with the thing that's most important in your life that you pushed for since you were five, you're failing. And I found myself questioning, do I really want to keep doing this? I had to get a hold of the self-pressure.

THE ENVIRONMENT FEELS MORE INDIVIDUALIZED THAN EVER, AND THE TEAM ATTITUDE IS TAKING A BACK SEAT TODAY. WHAT WOULD YOU TELL A YOUNG PLAYER COMING UP?

By looking at the name on the front of the uniform, not the name on the back, it just makes it a lot less complicated. If you're wasting energy pulling against someone and rooting against them, that's just a waste of brain power. It's so much more fun to win and do it together.

WE LEARNED THAT PRIDE OFTEN HAS A NEGATIVE CONNOTA-
TION, SUCH AS "PRIDE COMES BEFORE THE FALL." EXPLAIN
YOUR PERCEPTION OF THE DIFFERENCE BETWEEN "PRIDE"
AS COMPARED TO "BEING PROUD."

To me, pride is an attitude, it is the way you carry yourself,
which can be very negative. Being proud of your accomplishments is something to me that's more internal. You feel good
about what you have accomplished and no one else knows,
and no one else has to know. You can be proud of what you did.

WHAT DID YOU LEARN FROM THOSE FORMIDABLE DAYS AND
WHICH PEOPLE HAD THE MOST IMPACT?

You are never as bad as someone tells you are, and you are
never as good as someone tells you are. I think in our day of
social media, I always chuckle at things I see and things I read
because you can almost read most comments and understand if
someone's looking for affirmation or someone's looking for
attention or someone needs a pat on the back. You can tell just
by the things that they say.

*"Goals are different than desires. A goal many times takes the
help or assistance of someone else. You can have a goal of
doing that, but if you don't get your name put in the lineup and
you don't get enough at-bats, you're not going to reach your
goal. Did that mean you failed? No."*

– Matt Mieske

Be a Sponge

Learn from both the wins and the losses. Be a sponge and soak it all
up. One of my favorite people in the world is Alyson Hodson, the
CEO of a marketing firm in Edmonton, Alberta, in Canada. First, if
you make it in Edmonton, you are gritty! This is a town where

darkness pervades all winter and light all summer. It is beautiful with good people and a real sense of humility. Alyson is no different.

Her firm hired me to work with the group as a consultant and coach to upskill the leader and the team skills across the firm. Getting on the same page sounds easy, but it isn't. The concepts are simple, but the execution is not easy—a theme throughout this book.

One of the superpowers I discovered from Alyson is what most people would refer to as her gut instinct. People love that term, but I don't even believe in it. What I believe is that folks log their experiences mentally, physically, emotionally, and morally, and create standards and boundaries on future encounters and judgments they will have to make rapidly by discerning the data from the past, both good and bad, when confronted on similar situations based on an experience from the past. Alyson is amazing at this.

There are several issues with so-called gut instinct that can limit our skills at discernment in current challenges and for future ones. The first is poor memory. The second is having little knowledge of analytic assessment and skills, and the third is a quandary for many—often we only learn lessons from failure and negative experiences.

People typically learn less from winning but much more when they lose. A loss often means getting back to review the tapes asap, then getting back to training and figuring out how to win! Upon a victory, our time in review is little to none and often from a "glean the surface" perspective. People do not dive deeply into the victories, like they tend to do when they evaluate the losses, and the "how we find a way to win" mentality.

Alyson's specialty is that she learns from it all like a sponge. Her mind analyzes what went wrong, but also what went right. She internally logs all the data and has a clear perspective and recall for the data—both good and bad. It is impressive to see it in action and she does it effortlessly. It is like a supercomputer and AI rolled into a complex strategy.

How are you at learning, indexing, reviewing, extracting, compartmentalizing, and segregating data with precision in real time? Be a sponge and continue to develop your skills. If this is not your superpower, all is not lost. Pro tip: have a close, trusted advisor who has the skills and experience you need to take your team to the next level. This skill moves revenues up exponentially and can equally or sometimes exceedingly eliminate expenses to drop the value directly to your bottom line. Do not overlook this value in yourself or that team member—worth its weight in gold!

No One Is Coming

One of the big errors of my generation is that we have provided so very many safety nets for our children's generation. The whole society in my lifetime has become an exercise of safety analytics and so we must pull out certain playground equipment, limit speeds of quads, create rules for rules, and scare the snot out of everyone with how dangerous living is. I often wonder if statistically we are so much safer than we were before. I think if the improvement is minor, the juice has not been worth the squeeze. Having everyone walk around in fear of what *might* happen has done nothing for our society.

My generation likely has limited the resilience and determination of the following generations. Now, this is not with ill intent. It is one of those "careful what you wish for" scenarios. Our heart for protection and safety and the very intent of providing value likely did. But it also inadvertently created negative consequences—less resourcefulness, grit, resolve, stick-to-it-iveness, and more unintended consequences.

A mentality of "If it is to be, it is up to me" and one that is owning responsibility is crucial.

The "bail-out" method to soften the landing, as an approach, has been ineffective. No one is coming to save you. It is up to you. Whoever bailed you out in this life did not do you any favors.

Stay at the Top

The Alabama Crimson Tide are consistently rated as one of the top teams in college football. They have played for years at the top spot, or as one of the best teams. They won six national titles under the retired coach, Nick Saban, and that includes eight appearances and a decade-long winning percentage of .914. Every team tests where they stack up against the best when they play *any* team. For everyone else, this is a measuring stick of where they are and will be positioned to play their absolute best to see where they rank against the best. This is not the same mindset when playing a team that consistently is finishing under .500 and has not won a conference game in three years. With Coach Saban's retirement in early 2024, it will be interesting to see if Alabama can maintain their status as a top three team in the country year in and year out.

The Crimson Tide under Coach Saban reloaded and reran processes to maintain the highest standards. The standard was high for Coach Saban himself, the staff, the athletic department, players, coaches, video and team staff, medical staff, and any others associated with the program. He did not request it. He demanded it.

The mindset for building great processes for you to compete on the top levels every day is critical to consistent results.

If you do not have a mindset for "staying at the top," it will be difficult to remain there.

Still Learning

Be okay that your learning will be imperfect. I am still learning, and the best are always on this journey. I am not sure there is an end to this journey. What I have seen and know is that once a person learns the information, no one can take it away.

Key Takeaways

- Teaching someone else yields a retention rate above 90%, while listening to a lecture (5%) and reading (10%) still dominate our training.
- High retention rates correlate with coachability.
- Continuous improvement begins with an openness to learning.
- Find inspiration from a mentor, friend, or family member to be a better leader and person.
- Keep an open mind, stay humble, and be warned of pride.
- What brought success in the past may not be sufficient for future challenges.
- Embrace ongoing adaptation and growth in skills, knowledge, and character.

The Pain Exchange

Engage in hyper-learning, grow your network of influence, and upskill your game.

- Join a Peer Organization that can help you achieve the next level of development, such as the Entrepreneurs' Organization, Young Presidents' Organization, an executive forum, Vistage, Startup Grind, or the like.

    Most will have a cadence of learning via a forum or small group, which will be a *requirement* to attend monthly. Commit to the forum and the group learning events the organization offers.

    Peer group learning is like gym memberships; they are not spas. You are not going to get a massage and treatment with services rendered for your aches. This is a hardcore gym, and you are coming into this with the idea of getting in the best shape of your life and maximizing your performance. *You will have to do the work and put in the time to get the benefit.*

- Get an account with Audible, your local public library, Blink-ist, or areas of education from which you can get pointed content in a form that you can consume at a level where it will have the greatest impact for your development.

    Pro tip: One Blinkist benefit is the ability to synchronize your Evernote account (web based so you never lose a thought or idea again) with your Blinkist account so that when you go through a 15-minute review of a book, you can highlight your key learnings and takeaways, and those notes are captured in Evernote automatically. It is hyper-learning at the highest level.

14

24/7 Leadership

LEADERSHIP HAS CHANGED. I grew up at the tail end of the autocratic and authoritarian era of the Cold War and 1970s. Is it better? Is it worse? I'm not sure. And I don't think I'm qualified to make the assessment. I could debate both sides, and I would love to hear that argument sometime.

In the past, leaders were often quick to wield perceived power over others due to their position of authority or their title. This was common with teachers, coaches, music instructors, parents, and organizational leaders. Where it seemed a little less was our government leaders, who were likely afraid of being perceived as anything resembling their foreign counterparts, like Mussolini, Castro, and others.

Instead, a dictatorship often exists in micro ecosystems, like our homes, work teams, classes, private organizations, and youth sports. The leader sometimes leads with an all-knowing authoritarian style and barking orders despite modeling the behavior or having any semblance of self-awareness. "Do as I say, not as I do" is a common theme of the authoritarian style. And people may hold contempt for that attitude, but they align reluctantly.

People generally no longer align with this style of leadership. Higher standards have been set, with leaders who demand a lot of themselves and their team members, but build alignment with values, missions, and self-awareness. In other words, they "talk the talk, and walk the walk." People tend to find respect and admiration for leaders willing to lead by example and raise the standards, pushing the potential for each member of the organization.

Always On

Social media, accessibility from mobile phones, and the "plugged-in" generation being "always on" is an issue today. There is no anonymity anymore. Time stamps on posts, places, tagged people, and more are generated in this digital world, so that even the lowest-level inspection agent can build a timeline network of exactly where you have been, with whom, doing what, including the vehicles you've been in, the exact purchases made, at exactly the location and time, along with records of each activity during that time of what calls were made, to whom, the duration of those calls, and more.

If a leader goes out to the local grocery store at 11 p.m. to pick up something and then becomes entangled in a disagreement with someone checking out, an onlooker may record it and tag it on social media with some crazy headline like "CEO of local furniture manufacturing plant berates employee at local grocery store!" This will have 100,000 views before the CEO wakes up the next day to get ready for another day of navigating the challenging world of their business and the responsibilities they have to their 1,000 employees, hundreds of customers, family, and more. The previous day that person was an award-winning top executive thriving in a difficult environment and ultra-competitive business landscape, a parent to three children, a spouse of over 20 years, and an active member of the local community and church. Hours later they've been labeled another case of a power-driven person, with no empathy, a general disrespect for anyone below their status and education, an undesirable spouse, inhumane, and clearly a mean person who should never be allowed to lead any people, or even the local animal shelter!

Welcome to social media and 24/7 leadership. *You are always on.* Eyes are everywhere, and this is the issue with the double standard of accountability today. The very word "accountability" seems to feel like a curse word. It is a growing concern today. Most people want it for everyone else, but not for themselves.

I ask leaders why they want to be a leader. The answers vary from more money, to being driven to do it, or on their way to climbing the ladder of success. I tell them, "Be careful what you wish for." Leadership is hard.

Being authentic and genuine is key. If you are going to be on 24/7, you want to be assured that you can be who you want to be and show up as you are, without the judgment of others. There will still be challenges, unfortunately, but being authentic and genuine will help weather those storms.

A small percentage of people in leadership have left carnage in their wake due to extramarital affairs, drug use, overindulging in the things that will give a feeling of temporary enjoyment and a fleeting sense of satisfaction, only to find they are living with the pain of regret. And the pain is so deep that it is often followed by more of the same poor choices and behaviors that are likely to be outed by someone with a phone who has recorded this person's bad choices.

Lean Back In

Chad Curtis, Major League Baseball Player (retired); Two-Time World Series Championship with the Yankees; Christian College at GCU; Seven Years in Prison

I had the good fortune to coach Chad Curtis when I was with the Cleveland Indians. I knew he was a Michigander, having spent time there as a kid, and was a vocal University of Michigan football fan. We connected early due to our Michigan connection and similar experiences in our youth.

In my role as a strength and conditioning coach, I found Chad to be a dream of an athlete. Hard-charging, disciplined,

(continued)

(*continued*)

and intense, with a deep desire to succeed, he had a chip on his shoulder for being undersized and competing against the best in the world.

Chad professed his faith at nearly every opportunity and wanted better for everyone around him, and his effort to succeed and contribute to the success of the team was evident in everything he did. We call players like this "high-motor athletes." He is a doer and gets stuff done (GSD).

Chad was not likely to complain, was soft spoken, and clearly thoughtful. He was introverted, so when he spoke on matters that truly mattered to him, it surprised people, but they would listen.

As Chad and I sat down on *Winners Find a Way*, he was open to discussing the life of success, and his fall from grace, stories of restoration and redemption recognized by people of faith. How could one with so much discipline give into temptation in a moment of weakness? It's hard for some to understand, but I have been there myself. And it's hard to explain the "why" when we logically know it's wrong.

TRENT: AFTER FACING TOO MANY ADVERSITIES TO COUNT ON YOUR WAY TO THE MAJOR LEAGUES AND IN YOUR LONG-STANDING CAREER, WHERE DO YOU PIVOT TO TODAY TO YIELD THE IMPACT IN OTHERS' LIVES THAT YOU HAVE ALWAYS STRIVED TO HAVE?

Chad: In the back of my book, *In My Heart and on My Lips*, I share that I am actively involved in starting a nonprofit called Restore Ministries. And it is just about trying to bring some restoration from broken places, which I've had the opportunity to experience recently. I hope to take a pretty negative experience and turn it into something positive for myself and for other people who are struggling with similar things.

MANY PEOPLE WILL NOT KNOW ABOUT YOUR MINISTERING TO A DOOR ATTENDANT IN NEW YORK CITY OR SITTING WITH A YOUNG FAN AND TALKING ABOUT THEIR SPIRITUAL JOURNEY, PLUS THE COUNTLESS HOURS OF MODELING FOR OTHERS WHAT YOU BELIEVE TO BE WHAT STRONG FAITH LOOKS LIKE. DO YOU BELIEVE YOU ACHIEVED THE IMPACT?

I really believe that for a good portion of my major league baseball career, I tried to use my position as a baseball player to be an ambassador or representative of my faith.

Now, folks will judge you on a snippet of information, a quick meme, video, a headline, or interviews and articles of a few negative points in your life, and the dire consequences that followed.

LEADING YOUR AUTHENTIC LIFE AND SELF, YOU ALMOST LET THE JUDGMENT OF OTHERS TURN YOU INTO SOMETHING YOU DID NOT WANT TO BE, BUT YOU ADAPTED AND FACED THE NAYSAYERS, PULLED YOUR SHOULDERS BACK, RAISED YOUR CHIN, AND DECIDED SOMETHING DIFFERENT FOR YOUR LIFE. WHAT IS THE ROUTE TO OVERCOMING THE "ERROR OF YOUR WAYS"?

God has opportunity for me to use my baseball past, my failure, my prison experience, and my effort to move forward, and build Restore Ministries—if He wants to. I'm not gonna let the naysayers win, who caused me to build a cabin in the woods and just disengage from life. If He wants to use me moving forward, then I'm displaying my own restoration and being a part of other people's restoration.

> *"I was a David-type person trying to represent my faith in that environment. And I think that I was positive, but then you get to a point in your life where you just make some horrible choices and suffer the consequences of them."*
>
> *– Chad Curtis*

The "S" Word

Being around the top 1% of all performers in athletics and business is a blast and I am continually learning and humbled. One observation I have made over the years is that the top folks have a special mindset. They are resolute beyond compare and have a "never surrender" attitude and mindset.

Here is the challenge: everyone needs accountability in their life. Entrepreneurs do not typically have it, because they don't have a boss or someone to answer to unless they have mentors and/or are partially owned by an investment group. We all need accountability partners, and I dare say that each of us needs reminders that it is *not* all about us.

Making it to the top 1% is rare, and few make it that far. Once there, there are not people to talk to and it can become isolated and lonely. Plus, there is no one to bounce ideas off and further develop.

"As iron sharpens iron, so one person sharpens another."

– Proverbs 27:17

For those who need a peer group to fit into and find solace as a business owner, and leader, with fellow owners who have similar challenges as you, I recommend the Entrepreneurs' Organization, Vistage, Young Presidents' Organization, C-12, Convene, and many other groups. Here you will find like-minded individuals who are driven to succeed and have a great deal of pressure on them to provide not only for their own families, but their employees' families too. When an organization has 100 employees, the leader is really making decisions for 400 people, because the average household is four people. Find your path and direction, and then choose the group that is headed your way. After all, birds of a feather flock together.

Pride Comes Before the Fall

One of the top challenges for leaders is pride. Humility is an under-served master, and the lessons are expensive.

> "Before a downfall, the heart is haughty, but humility comes before honor. To answer before listening—that is folly and shame."
>
> **– Proverbs 18:12–13**

I have known many regrets and errors in my leadership journey, and for myself personally. Most people my age have at least five major events in their life where they regret the way they acted, or the decisions they made, or their chosen reaction to a situation. Alcohol often seems to have been an underlying factor in several of my friends' regrets, but that has not been my experience as I never have chosen to drink.

For me, my underlying challenge has been pride. In nearly every instance, an inflated and inaccurate sense of pride and ego was behind it. A poor response to a negative situation is like throwing kerosene on a fire, compounding an already unpleasant situation.

Who You Are and Where You Came From
Alan Nero, Springfield College Wrestling; MLB Agent

TV shows and movies depict certain characteristics and styles of agents, like *Jerry McQuire*, *Arliss*, and *Entourage's* super-agent, Ari Gold. Getting a chance to sit down with an MLB agent is something special. I have an exceptionally good friend who is related to Alan and so I was introduced. I was thrilled to sit down with the Octagon Agency's head of Major League Baseball!

Alan and I clearly have a great deal in common. He stud-ied at Springfield College, a school known as the birthplace of

(continued)

(*continued*)

basketball, and still renowned today for having a top physical education and exercise science program—which we both studied in college.

He is a former wrestler with an extremely diverse background in his agency work, plus he owns a top financial wealth management and insurance practice. Our common ground of sports and entrepreneurship had me super excited about this interview.

TRENT: WHAT IS YOUR PHILOSOPHY ON LEADING, GOALS, AND ACHIEVING SUCCESS?

Alan: I have a strong, adamant philosophy that life is a journey. Get on the train, enjoy the ride. If you're obsessed with a destination, you'll never get there. Just get on it, enjoy the ride, and experience it. And eventually get where you never dreamed you would go, which is what happened with me.

WHO HAD THE BIGGEST IMPACT ON YOUR JOURNEY? AND WHAT IS YOUR VIEW ON INTEGRITY?

Character is doing the right thing, when no one knows, but that way you can sleep good at night. So if you want to know who the greatest influence is on me, by far it was my dad.

WHAT HAS BEEN YOUR SUPERPOWER AND SEPARATOR FOR YOU TO ACHIEVING SUCCESS?

God doesn't give you everything. You could be the best left-handed pitcher who ever lived, and it doesn't mean you have a great personality. You can be the greatest hitter who ever lived; it doesn't mean that people like you. And so I have something in my nature and in my personality where people gravitate to me. And it's a blessing, sometimes it's a curse, because it's a lot of responsibility.

WHAT WOULD BE YOUR BEST ADVICE FOR THOSE ON THEIR WAY TO GREATNESS, AND THAT YOU GIVE YOUR CLIENTS?

So the one thing I have tried to continue to remind my clients is, don't forget who you are and where you came from.

There is a substantial difference between the average successful ordinary businessperson in a suit and an extraordinarily successful star athlete. The difference is that there is a certain amount of anonymity that the normal successful businessperson can have.

BASEBALL FEELS LIKE IT HAS CHANGED FROM WHEN WE WERE KIDS AND PLAYERS STAYED WITH THE SAME TEAM FOR A LONG TIME. WHAT ARE SOME OF THE CHALLENGES FOR TODAY'S ATHLETES AND THE GAME?

It is hard because loyalty should cut both ways. But people who are so committed to loyalty, somehow that becomes their greatest weakness. And I've struggled with that in the past. It is something that is not a natural thing to do. But you have to do it.

HOW DO YOU MEET TEAM MEMBERS AND FOLKS WHERE THEY ARE? AND HOW DO YOU CONTINUE TO MOTIVATE THEM?

It is something that when you are trying to provide that leadership, you have to be sensitive to it and you have to act quickly. They say the most expensive time in a boss's life is when an employee could have gotten a raise and has to come to you and ask for that raise. Because basically, that employee had to feel totally unappreciated and had to wait and come in and literally begged. And they say that's the most expensive time in a manager's life.

It is the same thing on the opposite side. If you see someone who doesn't buy in, and someone who's not having a

(continued)

(*continued*)

positive impact, you need to make that decision. That's been difficult for team members.

WE HEAR PEOPLE SAY THAT YOU BECOME THE FIVE PEOPLE YOU SURROUND YOURSELF WITH AND SPEND THE MOST TIME WITH. WHAT IS YOUR STANCE ON THAT?

You want to surround yourself with the best—the best in the world. But if that's the case, you have to be the best yourself. So we have that same commitment to excellence.

"Well, you have to set an example, you have to limit yourself, you cannot expect someone to buy into something that you don't live."

– *Alan Nero*

The Responsibility Journey

Alan touched on his feelings of carrying the weight of responsibility for his clients and being a person people gravitate toward. He clearly does not take his role and impact lightly. Unfortunately, many do.

To be a successful leader, you must understand that responsibility for yourself, your family, your team members, your clients, your vendors, and others comes with the territory. Often it is said that a leader will pass the credit and take the blame.

I'm Responsible and I Care

Tonya Lanthier, College Basketball Player; Founder, Dental Post; Entrepreneur

Tonya and I met serving our respective local board of directors for the Entrepreneurs' Organization (EO). For me it was Chicago, and she was adding impact for Atlanta.

Tonya has energy and excellent focus. Her intensity to compete is palpable. Having known her as a peer in EO for several years now, I welcomed her to *Winners Find a Way* as she was in the middle of selling the business she had built up.

TRENT: HOW DO YOU FIND THE ENERGY TO LEAD, BE A MOM, COMMIT TO SO MANY OTHERS, BE CHARITABLE, AND STAY SUPER FIT, AND WHAT IS DRIVING YOU?

Tonya: I've always had the mindset of performing at an Olympic level. Create something bigger than yourself. My grandparents take care of people and those values really stuck with me. It wasn't that they made me work. I learned to work.

WHAT WOULD YOU TELL A LEADER BATTLING IMPOSTER SYNDROME AND INTERNAL CHALLENGES?

I think that you really have to sit with yourself and be happy with who you are. And when you come to that place where you're happy with just being you, I think that's where it has to come from within.

Our limiting belief system or patterns and the kind of things that we are expecting are important. I've never been the victim. And I've always seen people for what they are, not what I want them to be. And I will say, I was mad, and I was angry as a child, when all that was going on with my dad. And I didn't know where that was coming from at the time. And I had to move through the process to get to the other side and see the beauty in it. But we're not born with a manual of how to be, or how to raise children, or whatnot. I always tell my kids, I'm not perfect, I don't expect you to be perfect.

WHAT DO YOU THINK YOUR SUPERPOWERS ARE AS A LEADER?

I can see patterns and understand people and what their underlying motivation is. And I care, I think. I am responsible, and

(continued)

(*continued*)

I care. And I think that I see patterns and how "the what" for people gets in people's way. And I ask myself all the time, "What is getting in my way right now? To get what I want, what is in my way right now? Where am I not balanced? What am I not seeing?" And then I'll seek out someone and go, "Give me some feedback. Tell me what I cannot see in myself." I also plan what I want. I can design in my head what I want. I can see it.

I think my wealth right now is to be able to do what I want with my time. I think time is the currency. While you can always make more money, you can't make more time. I am very efficient with my time.

WHAT HAVE YOU SEEN AS A MAJOR CHALLENGE FOR LEADERS?

I think people let things irritate them more than they should. And I think you should always ask; "Does it really matter? Is this going to matter?" My grandmother used to say, "Is that going to matter?" It's like toilet paper, for example. If it's over or under, does it really matter? Because it gets the job done.

"My will to succeed is greater than my fear."

– Tonya Lanthier

Fearmongers

I have no tolerance for people who want to scare folks and create a level of power over them. Fear is a power play and when used over others, it should not be tolerated. For any folks who have been in situations of abuse—and that is most of us—there is a power dynamic. I believe that is why abused people abuse people. Or hurt people hurt people.

I was sexually abused as a young boy. It lasted a brief period over what I would guess is a few intermittent events over a few years, from when I was four to seven years old.

Someone took away my control and my power and my freedoms and used that to get what they wanted. This results in a victim mentality in those who have been subjected to such treatment. And the challenge is that we know exactly what it feels like to be under someone else's control and we do not like it. Conditioning and self-preservation preclude us from seeing how we ourselves might be guilty of the same behavior in some fashion.

I have been through counseling and find it beneficial not only to address how my past has shaped me, but also because it helps me recognize that I may not think the same as someone who has not been through the same things, and that is okay. Self-awareness has been particularly important, and always having a trusted counselor to speak with on these matters has always helped me.

Fear will sap the confidence right from your body and will continue to do so if you hold on to the fear and fail to address it head on.

I hear leaders say things like "The stress I was under at that age and how poorly I was treated is nothing compared to how easy everyone around here has it now." Yet, in the same breath, the person is using their status as a controlling, self-serving leader who remains human: "I want what I want, and I deserve it because I have earned it." Consideration for others is not factored in, but it is not intentional. Do not believe yourself to be a bad person because this is happening in your world. It is a human condition. Building awareness about this is one of the greatest strengths of a world-class leader.

When people choose to instill fear in you in whatever form or modality, ask yourself, "What's in it for them?" Fear is not about you; it is about control. Do not *ever* give up your power. You decide what you're willing to let in.

"I spent 90% of my life worried about things that never happened."

– Mark Twain

Sports Teach Responsibility

Owning our responsibility is a part of any journey and should be learned from the time we are young, and sports is a catalyst for training in this. The challenge is that in team sports where success is linked to many, it is sometimes difficult to pinpoint the direct correlation between the success, the challenges, and the failures.

Individual sports such as swimming, wrestling, tennis, bowling, gymnastics, archery, or diving are fabulous ways for athletes to discover responsibility. I recommend all parents enroll their kids in at least one single-person sport or recreation that will allow them to develop self-control and an understanding of the training and shaping of personal responsibility.

"You are responsible for your results."

– Stephen M. R. Covey

Key Takeaways

- Leaders are "on" all the time.
- Be authentic and genuine for effectiveness.
- Lean into your failures and shortcomings and don't hide errors or mistakes.
- Know when to yield and when to stand firm.
- Join a network where iron sharpens iron for personal and professional development.
- Effective leaders make disciplined choices and avoid regrets.
- Find good mentors and role models, play to your strengths, and remember where you came from.

- You are responsible for your results.
- Foster a positive and effective team environment.

The Pain Exchange

Direct your steps on all input and output and have a plan for both. What are you allowing in?

Input Plan: Limit your time with social media. If it's important to your work, have a team member vet your incoming posts and data on your phone and all social media channels, filter your laptop, and limit inboxes and channels for how folks can reach you. Have an assistant manage your email, or pay a professional group. It's more affordable than you think and takes tons of pressure off you.

What do you want to contribute to others?

Output Plan: If you can, pay a professional, or have a team, to manage *all* your outgoing content, except email. Your marketing person can turn alarms off on your social media, and even eliminate or hide you from seeing messages and comments on posts. Have an outgoing edit software check messages and verify before any go out. Set rules and boundaries to lock down apps during certain times.

Advanced Pain Exchange

Buy a supervised system for web surfing, like Covenant Eyes, for all devices.

Get a privacy glass cover for your phone and laptop/tablet.

Meet a mentor or counselor every month for 45 minutes or longer.

About the Author

Trent M. Clark is an internationally acclaimed keynote speaker and one of the world's foremost thought leaders on leadership development, cultural growth, building and leading winning teams, and mentorship. His energy and insights on leadership, culture, and organizational performance originated from his years coaching in professional baseball with some of the most acclaimed coaches of all time, and being part of teams that went to three World Series—including the 2002 World Champion Los Angeles Angels of Anaheim!

In business, Coach Trent has honed his skills of servant leadership through the franchising system of 1-800-Got-Junk? with Brian Scudamore and Cameron Herald, plus the Entrepreneurs' Organization, serving both in local and global leadership capacities. He also has started and built 12 brands and organizations in fitness, marine transport, government contracting, NIL education, and leadership development and consulting.

Coach Trent also serves as a trusted advisor to many small to medium businesses from the entrepreneurial community that regularly double the valuation of their business . . . fast!

Coach Trent's journey to success began on the tennis court as a ranked junior player and a baseball player, later playing both sports at the University of Toledo. His journey to excellence was paved by some of the best coaches in the world, like Sparky Anderson, Nick Saban, Tom Izzo, Bobby Magallanes, Mike Butcher, Don Wakamatsu, Mike Scioscia, Ty Van Burkleo, Joe Maddon, Mike Hargrove, Bud Black, and more.

Coach Trent resides in West Michigan with his wife of 29 years, where they have five kids, a daughter-in-law, and a grandson. In his work, he never stops learning to enable teams to thrive and enjoy their work together and create massive impact across the globe!

WE WOULD LIKE to connect with you by SMS to keep you connected on all things leadership. Click the QR code and just send the text to get started.

Index